FINANCIAL INSTITUTIONS AND SERVICES

FINANCIAL MARKETS

A GUIDED TOUR

Financial Institutions and Services

Additional books in this series can be found on Nova's website
under the Series tab.

Additional E-books in this series can be found on Nova's website
under the E-book tab.

Economic Issues, Problems and Perspectives

Additional books in this series can be found on Nova's website
under the Series tab.

Additional E-books in this series can be found on Nova's website
under the E-book tab.

FINANCIAL INSTITUTIONS AND SERVICES

FINANCIAL MARKETS

A GUIDED TOUR

MANEL ANTELO
AND
DAVID PEON

Nova Science Publishers, Inc.
New York

For permission to use material from this book please contact us:
Telephone 631-231-7269; Fax 631-231-8175
Web Site: http://www.novapublishers.com

NOTICE TO THE READER

Additional color graphics may be available in the e-book version of this book.

LIBRARY OF CONGRESS CATALOGING-IN-PUBLICATION DATA

Financial markets: a guided tour / editors, Manel Antelo, David Peon.
p. cm.
Includes index.
ISBN 978-1-62100-096-9 (hardcover)
1. Financial institutions. 2. Capital market. I. Antelo, Manel. II. Peon, David, 1976-
HG4523.F558 2011
332.64--dc23

2011031028

Published by Nova Science Publishers, Inc. † New York

To Susana and Sarah M. A.

Para María e Anxo D. P.

CONTENTS

LIST OF TABLES

LIST OF FIGURES

FOREWORD

If there were still any doubts, as a result of the crisis, which began in the summer of 2007 and had not ended at the beginning of 2011, everyone is now convinced, first abruptly and then painfully, of the extraordinary importance of financial markets in people's lives and activities. For good or bad, consecrated by some and demonized by others, the markets have become key pillars of modern economies.

Back in 2007, we should remember that only a very few 'initiated' people knew about the existence of an enormous volume of financial operations, based on subprime mortgages with a high probability of not being paid, which were packaged as prime quality fixed-income issues designed by wizards in the financial sector and sold to the cleverest fund managers. To a large extent, the crisis has made it clear that financial knowledge, such an important aspect of our economies and our environment, is scant. Perhaps because almost no one, including consumers and providers for different reasons, had much interest in changing the situation.

The time has come to tackle the dissemination of financial knowledge from a new, rigorous and solid scientific perspective. Contrary to what is commonly believed, the body of scientific theory developed in the financial sphere over the last fifty years is very rich and its influence on the real world is enormous compared to that of other social sciences. But the application of this theory by economic agents has not followed a satisfactory path. Why? Probably for three reasons. First, converting the rich body of theory into rules that can be understood and applied has not been an easy task. Second, there are significant conflicts of interest in the functioning of financial markets. Third, the appropriate incentives to encourage the dissemination of financial knowledge have yet to be found.

There is still much to be done to disseminate the academic discoveries in finances among professionals (yes professionals) and investors. This is a challenge that some, including the authors of this book, intend to face.

What we call financial markets are today a broad series of private and public institutions and companies, rules and systems of trading, brokers, technical, operating and organisational systems which can no longer be understood outside a global context. They have reached a very high level of development and complexity and fundamentally fulfil two enormously important functions: they channel finance and they determine the price of instruments through which this finance is channelled.

Among the large array of financial markets written about in this book are some which are very close to being the reference of what 'markets' should be and toward which all markets, not only financial, should move. The magnitude of transactions and the large number of participants reached over the last few decades have made them in some cases 'almost perfect' or very 'efficient'. The most rigorous scientific evidence and the very experience of investors shows that some financial markets are increasingly efficient, backed by a majority rational performance, growing transparency and the speed with which information is transmitted. This efficiency makes the fluctuation of markets close to a random walk and configures a very complex scenario for investors and fund managers when it comes to making investment decisions. To make things even more complex, the emergence of a body of scientific knowledge, known as behavioural finance, has revealed psychological features when investors and managers take investment decisions.

These are just some examples of the difficulty of relating scientific discoveries with the practice of the markets and investment in financial products. Scrutinising this way and, in some cases, creating it is clearly the appropriate path, and this is the view of the authors of this tour of the financial markets who, on the basis of solid foundations in scientific evidence, make this knowledge available to investors and professionals.

Domingo J. García-Coto
Head of the Research Department
BME (Spanish Exchanges)

ACKNOWLEDGMENTS

The source of this book is two-fold. On one hand, the lecture notes used through years of classes; on the other, a long professional interaction with colleagues. We have been fortunate to have these points of departure in preparing the book. Because of this we would like to thank those who have discussed the content with us at various stages in the development of the book. All of them provided us useful advice and criticism that greatly improved our work, challenging our ideas as well. Our most significant debts go to Anxo Calvo for a great deal of support in the Academics, and for his teachings in corporate finance in particular. We are also indebted to Juan C. Estévez, David García, Antonio Martínez, Alexandre Pedrosa and Marcos Vizcaíno, for helping with some of the diagrams; and to Cristina Anido, Fernando de Llano and Marcos Vizcaíno once again, for our work together preparing the subjects to teach our students on financial markets. We hope the final product meets with their approval.

Our students who have used several parts of this book have been very generous and insightful with their time and provided numerous comments in early drafts of the manuscript. Many of their suggestions helped us to improve the book and thus they have been incorporated into the final product.

We would also like to thank several people at Nova Science Publihers, Inc. for their support of this project at its final stage. We have received enthusiastic assistance from them to the point that they have been an exceptional partner. Very special thanks to Nadya S. Gotsiridze-Columbus, President of Nova Science Publishers, Inc., as well as Carra Feagaiga and Jennifer Ramirez, from Department of Acquisitions at Nova Science Publishers, Inc.

Our final thanks are devoted to our wives and children, Susana, María, Sarah, and Anxo. Scarce time was reallocated away from them to complete this work. Or, without subterfuge, they were unfailingly patient and understanding while we were in the learning process about economics and finance.

M.A.
D.P.

June, 2011

INTRODUCTION

On September 11th, 2001, the world was stunned by terrorist attacks on American soil. A decade before we had witnessed the fall of communism, so with the end of the confrontation that characterized the Cold War and with the emergence of a globalized world that followed, a long period of peace time and prosperity was expected. Some people claimed the 'end of History', but for a world living under such paradigm, waking up one day watching live on TV the greatest military power on Earth under attack at its own land was stunning

But it was during another month of September, this time September 2008, when probably our view of the world changed the most. We had considered ourselves living in a long-term no-end-in-sight prosperity era, when most societies from either Western, former Soviet or new emerging countries had entered into a period of Great Moderation characterised by steady growth, smooth business cycles, low inflation, increasing confidence in the future performance of the economy and, therefore, a lower risk perception by most economic agents. Again, for a world living under such paradigm, waking up one day witnessing Wall Street icons such as Lehman Brothers, Merrill Lynch or AIG plummeting within just 24 hours, watching the once untouchable monetary policymakers both in the U.S. and the Eurozone unable to take control of the situation, the Bush Administration assuming they had no other option than intervene in the market economy to rescue the banking system—and so they did many governments of any ideology around the world—and finally, witnessing stock markets losing almost two thirds of their value in the middle of the financial panic within the months following left all of us, from authorities to common people, completely thunderstruck.

Perhaps the worldwide financial meltdown had not the visual impact the terrorist attacks over the New York's World Trade Centre had, but promptly common people had their 'dose of reality' when they experienced in their own lives the consequences of the global financial panic: credit shortage to households and companies, loss of wealth due to huge market falls both in the financial and real estate markets, massive loss of jobs and company profits and, to sum up, the worst economic downturn in decades.

All these events have raised interest, both in the academic world and at Main Street, on financial markets, their role in the economy and how to ensure their correct functioning for the good development of our economies. Economists and policymakers have focused most of their efforts in analyzing what has happened and which regulations should be implemented in order to avoid that it could happen again. The so-called re-foundation of capitalism will probably not be such a deep transformation, but one should not underestimate the importance of changes to come in areas like banking regulation, unregulated derivatives markets or the coordination among governments and financial authorities all over the world, where the Group of Twenty (G-20) is probably the most important example.

We, as authors of this book, are particularly concerned about dealing with what we feel is a growing interest on understanding financial markets among people on Main Street. We mean to bring financial markets closer to anyone interested in them, regardless of their knowledge on economic or financial topics. We have paid special attention to make its reading as enjoyable as possible, so in order to make it possible no high mathematical skills or expertise on financial markets are required.

Financial markets are the places or mechanisms that connect savers and investors interested in trading financial assets, determining their prices. These include basically capital markets, where companies and governments get from investors the financing they need in form of bonds, shares and other securities, and money markets, where money and other short term liquid assets are traded providing means of payment, hence enhancing the liquidity of the system. Furthermore, financial markets also provide agents with means to operate internationally through currency markets and to hedge risks (or speculate with them, if they are willing) through the derivatives markets.

In this book we examine the functioning of all of these markets. To this end, part I of the book is devoted to the analysis of financial markets—what they are and how do they work—so the reader can understand the crucial role these markets play on a modern economy. The correct understanding of such role requires the full comprehension of key issues like the origins of money and financial system, their functions, the control of stock of money, the role banks play in the economy as well as that of all financial markets (money, debt, equity, currency, derivatives and alternative markets). This in turn obliges to understand the basics of money and financial system, which types of instruments are negotiated in them, by which market participants and what for. Put differently, to examine markets as venues where economic agents look for financing. In such way, classical taxonomy distinguishes between money markets (which provide means of payment) and capital markets (which provide long-term financing) at first level, whereas inside capital markets we differentiate between external financing (debt markets) and self financing (equities) on a second level. Therefore, on financial markets banks, states, corporations, intermediaries, and many other private and public agents issue securities and sell them to other market participants in exchange for the financing required. However, derivatives, alternative investments and currency markets account for other purposes, such as hedging risks, speculate or investing abroad.

We must realize then that no financial markets would exist if there were no investors interested in buying such bonds, money assets, equities or derivatives. Financial markets offer a universe of investment alternatives to those agents with excess savings available. Any investor facing all these alternatives would first wonder which forces guide financial markets, and after answering that question she would look for the investment procedures and allocation that better suit her objectives.

Therefore, in part II, we are going to examine how investors approach financial markets and which indicators they consider in their investment decisions. Besides, we will also provide a brief description of some study areas, such as portfolio management theory, asset pricing models, fundamental analysis, technical analysis, psychology of financial markets and behavioural finance which offer investment solutions that help market participants when facing their decision making process.

Perhaps readers would agree that a book about financial markets written these days should not left out the details concerning the origins of the Great Recession that began on August 2007 and affects Western economies mainly. To fulfil that goal, we devote part III of the book to offer our view on the causes and consequences of the financial meltdown and the Great Recession following.

Starting from the years of the so-called 'Great Moderation', when risk aversion in our societies fell to the minimum level, the main goal of this part is twofold. First, to analyse the basic 'antecedents' that led to the financial meltdown, namely the credit expansion and the housing boom in most Western economies, the speculative use of derivatives on a massive scale, a long period of—probably not justified—low interest rates, especially in the U.S. economy, and the substantial global imbalances generated during the last two decades of globalization. Second, to offer a step-by-step explanation on how the financial meltdown occurred, as well as the consequences of the Great Depression that followed.

All of these topics are examined in the journey the book you have in your hands takes. Needless to say we would be very pleased if you come along with us in this travel across financial markets. You are warmly invited.

PART I: FINANCIAL MARKETS: WHAT THEY ARE AND WHAT THEY ARE FOR

What are financial—money and capital—markets for? How do they work? This part of the book begins by addressing these and other related topics so readers are able to understand the crucial role these markets play on modern economies. The correct understanding of such role requires the full comprehension of key issues like the origins of money and financial system, their functions, the control of stock of money, the role banks play in the economy as well as that of all financial markets (money, debt, equity, currency, derivatives and alternative markets). This in turn obliges to understand the basics of money and financial system, which types of instruments are negotiated in them, by which market participants and what for.

To this end, part I is organized in five chapters as follows. In chapter 1 we survey the historical perspective of financial markets: how financial markets emerged, starting from the origins of money and the first forms it took, until the most recent development of the derivatives markets. Readers will find there a wide description of this evolution that shall make them understand why financial markets are so essential today in capitalist economies and how they have helped to our economic progress. In particular, we address four main issues: first, the origins of money; second, the origins of the fiduciary money and the banking system; third, how economies can be regulated through money supply; and fourth, the way financial markets other than money markets appeared in modern economies. In chapter 2 we deal with the money markets, paying special attention on how economic authorities regulate the level of money supply under a fractionary-reserve banking system. Chapters 3 and 4 are devoted to the analysis of capital markets, in particular debt securities in chapter 3 and equity markets in chapter 4. Finally, in chapter 5 we provide a wide description of currency markets, derivatives markets, as well as other alternative investments.

Chapter 1

A HISTORICAL VIEW OF FINANCIAL MARKETS

Financial markets play an essential role in capitalist economies. Any market economy requires a financial system through which savings and investments are conveyed, that allows risks to be transferred from one party to another, and that offers participants with vehicles to store their wealth. Some economic agents[1], for example, are in need to finance their activities, so they raise capital issuing financial assets that are sold to market participants with surplus savings in exchange of some return[2]. Other agents, on the other hand, face different forms of risk that they are willing to insure against by, for instance, buying a derivatives contract[3]. And in any case, financial markets offer a means to price securities in a way they provide accurate signals for allocation of the economy's capital stock, which, in words of Eugene Fama[4], is the primary role of capital markets.

Financial assets—also known as 'securities'—represent an asset to its buyer and a liability to its issuer. For such reason, whereas the production of a real asset increases wealth in an economy, the emission of a security itself it does not (since any financial asset represents a liability to another economic agent). But financial markets provide economies with the essential function of mobilizing real resources and offering insurance for the various forms of risk. This way, at money markets[5] all economic agents, both private and public, can raise short-term funds whereas through capital markets they can raise long-term funds for their investments. Furthermore, through money markets, Central Banks—such as the European Central Bank, the Fed[6] in the U.S., the Bank of England in U.K. or the Bank of

[1] Basic economic agents would be individuals and families, enterprises, financial institutions and the Government.

[2] For example we may think of a company in any economic sector. It might choose to issue either new shares or corporate bonds, which shall be defined and described in chapters 4 and 3, respectively, and sell them to willing investors in order to raise capital. This way, the company gets the capital necessary to finance its activities, and the investors get a return for their savings

[3] Think for instance of a person that has to make monthly payments on her mortgage. If payments are set such that they are variable through time–because for example they are related to some interest rate such as Libor or Euribor–perhaps she would be concerned whether interest rates may rise in the future, making regular payments more expensive. One alternative for this person to insure against this possibility would be buying any of the different types of derivatives contracts, which are defined and described in section 5.2, available in the derivatives markets.

[4] See Fama (1970).

[5] Financial markets are classified as money markets and capital markets–according to the maturity of the securities traded in them–as we shall see later in this section.

[6] The 'Fed' is the short name for the Federal Reserve, i.e. the U.S. Central Bank.

Japan in Japan— regulate the quantity of money in our economies, which is one of the most important policies governments have to promote a consistent and smooth economic growth. And above all, financial markets help investors matching their needs by putting in contact those who need to raise capital with those who have it, transferring risks from agents who want to avoid them to those who are willing to take them, and improving liquidity of the system.

As we will be seeing throughout this part of the book, in financial markets the economic agents trade a whole array of securities, ranging from money in all its forms, equity securities or debt issues of both sovereign States and private agents, to the most sophisticated derivatives and hedge funds. Hence, in order to get a first insight of how all of them evolved into what they are today, and which role they play in the economy, we will make it better by taking a historical approach: how did it all began?

1.1. Money and Its Origins

> "Money, it's a crime. Share it fairly, but don't take a slice of my pie"
> 'Money'—Pink Floyd

Long ago (and not so long, too) when market economies began, trade was conducted through barter, that is, paying for goods and services with other goods and services, instead of with money[7]. To illustrate, a farmer specialized in producing apples could only buy some milk for her own consumption by directly exchanging both goods at the market. And this implied buyer and seller (two farmers) should have their properties ready to trade at the same time, and physically take them to the market for exchange. It is hard to imagine how barter could work today, especially considering the importance of the services sector in modern economies and the fact that it does not produce physical goods.

Money was created in order to facilitate trade: when the farmer has her apples available, she can trade them for money. Later, when she wants to buy some milk, she can spend the money she has earned. All this may look pretty obvious, but readers should be aware of two important issues. The first one is that in any transaction, money appears—in all of its forms—by the same value of the goods or services being traded. Indeed, commerce led to the emergence of financial markets, closely related to the real economy as a mirror image of it. The second issue is a question: what shall we use as money? We should use anything that is generally accepted as payment, but... which features should that good have in order to be 'generally accepted'?

For centuries, some different commodities were used as money. To avoid the inconveniences of barter, those commodities should be valuable, non-perishable, cumulative and easy to transport. We can still see it as a form of barter, but definitely it is easier to sell apples for salt—an example of goods that were once used as money[8]—and keep then the salt stored until the farmer needed or could afford milk.

This way, the two most important properties of money appeared from the very beginning: as a medium of exchange—buyers can give it to sellers to pay for goods and services—and as

[7] Indeed, barter becomes quite popular in those cases in which the quality of money is low or at least uncertain, there is high inflation or counterfeiting, people are asset-rich but cash-poor, taxation is very high, etc.

[8] In fact the word 'salary' comes from its use during the Roman Empire.

a store of value—it can be used to transfer purchasing power into to the future. And the other two properties from the classical definition of money we will see later—unit of account and standard of deferred payment—derived from the utility of the two former ones.

Soon, silver and gold were used as common currencies. In Greece, Rome, the Renaissance... and even in the twentieth century, gold and other precious metals were used as money. They met the features required: they were valuable, non perishable, easy to transport and to accumulate, and hence they could be used to trade in commerce and to store wealth. But as the use of money spread, one definitive feature proved decisive: money should be something you could rely on, something you could trust.

1.2. Fiduciary Money or the Origins of Banking System

As Freixas and Rochet pointed out[9],

> [...] Greek word for bank (trapeza) designated the balance that early money changers used to weigh coins in order to determine the exact quantity of precious metal the coins contained.

This sentence gives us a clue on the origins of the banking system: the first concern about money as its use spread was to make sure not to be deceived. That is, our farmer should be given the exact quantity she was expecting, not less. One can imagine that with the emergence of money also came the first financial swindlers, people trying to falsify its value, and merchants were concerned about that. Therefore, one feature of precious metals as an optimal medium of exchange (to be valuable) was also the first reason for the banking system to appear.

[M] Quentin Metsys – Le Prêteur et sa Femme (1514).

[9] Freixas and Rochet (1997), p. 3.

Another characteristic of money as a medium of exchange (to be cumulative) implied as well the necessity to store it safely, in order to reduce the risk of loss or robbery. Soon banks assumed this role, too. Goldsmiths were probably the first businesses to accept deposits of metals in their vaults, and their clients received depository notes in return. Those notes, just pieces of paper indeed, early played for transaction purposes the same role as the gold they represented. Bank notes, the most widespread form of payment until our days, were born this way.

Banks built a reputation by making payments with 'good-quality money', proving their deposits were riskless, providing liquidity between different currencies (national and foreign money exchanging, for instance), and facilitating the transfer of funds for payments from one person's account to others'. Whenever a bank showed it was able to perform reliably and safely, merchants paid and accepted payments using notes from that bank. Whenever a bank did not proved so, it failed—and probably a bank run[10] would take place.

'Fides', the Latin word for faith, was crucial behind these relationships. And money used in those transactions—bank notes with no intrinsic value, just the faith in a promise to be given 'good money' back from the issuer at first claim—received the name of 'fiduciary money'. Fiduciary money was indeed cumulative and easy to transport, but was not valuable itself. Faith played that role, so a commodity that met all the properties required (medium of exchange, store of value, unit of account and standard of deferred payment) without being valuable ended being used as money. This historical step—the passage from a commodity to worldwide accepted fiduciary money—is probably the most enigmatic process in capitalist societies not only to economists, but to philosophers and sociologists too. It is essential for our readers to understand and keep in mind this fiduciary nature of financial markets, because this fact explains both the extraordinary development they have achieved in Western capitalist economies as well as their inherent instability.

1.3. Regulating the Economy through Money Supply

Through history, all governments around the world retained the right to issue currency to themselves. Kings kept the right of 'seignorage', that is, the net revenue derived from the issuing of money: since there is a difference between the face value of a coin and the cost of producing it, whoever who has that right would have a return for free.

Together with their armies, government institutions and so on, the right to issue money has been one of the instruments governments have based their power. When kings run out of money because of their debts, they financed their next war by simply printing more money. But pretty soon they realized this behaviour led only to inflation! As the economist Irving Fisher[11] would show centuries later, controlling the supply of money within a country is essential, since money should be closely related to the real economy as a mirror image of it, and if not, it only produces an imbalance. This is formally expressed through the so-called quantity theory of money as

---

[10] A bank run is a synonym for bank panic, a situation that occurs when clients of such bank believe the institution is at risk–whether they are right or not–so they start withdrawing their money there at the same time.

[11] Fisher (1911).

$$M \cdot V = P \cdot T, \quad (1)$$

where M denotes the stock of money in the economy, V the number of times money changes hands (or the velocity of circulation of money as is known in the economic jargon)[12], P stands for the average price level and T for the number of transactions in the economy.

Fisher's equation stated in (1) states that if the velocity of money and the volume of transactions are both constant, at least in the short-run, then any change in the money supply of a currency leads directly to a change in prices. Any increase in M would only lead to an increase in P. In words, printing money generates only inflation and has no positive effect over the wealth of a nation or, in the economic jargon, money is neutral. This theory was accepted until the 1930s when the British economist John M. Keynes pointed out that an increase in the money supply seemed to lead to a fall in the velocity of circulation and to an increase in real income (once inflation is considered). Later, economists such as American Milton Friedman assumed that V could change in response to variations in M, but only in stable, predictable way that did not challenged the validity of the quantity theory. At present, the controversy continues.

Once the link between stock of money, economic growth and inflation was revealed, regulating the economy through money supply has proved essential. The Bank of England's early days provide a good example: it had a weather vane (still there today) to provide a forecast of demand for money. How did it work? Changes in the direction and the speed of the wind gave them accurate predictions about when ships, laden with commodities to trade, would arrive to London up the river Thames. It was the Bank of England duty to provide the economy with the correct amount of money for neither inflation nor pressure over demand for commodities would exist[13].

From the 18th century to the second half of the 20th notes and coins issued by most Western economies were backed by gold. It was the so-called 'gold standard', a monetary system where the unit of account is a fixed weight of gold. To illustrate, in 1944 the agreements of monetary management signed in Mount Washington Hotel of Bretton Woods (New Hampshire, U.S.) set the convertibility of the U.S. dollar at $35 per ounce, while all the other currencies pegged to the U.S. dollar with the promise of the U.S. Treasury to pay that amount in gold at first demand. The gold standard, apart from being severely affected by Gresham's Law[14], generated numerous economic crisis through history—for instance, it is argued by some researchers and analysts that it limited the ability of central banks to expand money supply during the Great Depression (1929-1939), prolonging its damages. So finally this system proved untenable, mainly because if everyday our economies are getting bigger and bigger, we produce more and more goods, we are a growing number of people inhabiting planet Earth, but we require all commercial transactions to be backed by gold or silver... eventually it does not matter how much ore mines can produce, there will not be enough gold supply in this world. That is why it is amazing to realize that gold standard was still maintained indirectly after the World War II, and was not finally abandoned until... August

---

[12] Technically, it is approximated as gross domestic product divided by the money supply.

[13] Read the story at <http://cms.cass.cn/show_News_e.asp?id=9769>.

[14] An expression coined by British economist Henry Macleod–named 'Gresham's Law after Sir Thomas Gresham– expresses the empirical evidence that, in the absence of legal-tender currencies, metal coins made of precious metals are thrown out of the market by counterfeit currencies (a mix made of the original precious metal and another of lower quality). In Gresham's words, 'bad money drives out good'.

1971! when Richard Nixon, the President of the U.S. at the time, ended the convertibility of the dollar to gold due mainly to two facts; the achievement of the pick in the U.S.'s oil production that converted that country from an exporting oil into a net importing oil, and Vietnam's War expenditures.

Today, governments had ceded control over most of the money supply to private banks. Through the so-called fractional-reserve banking system, banks create money through credit so the money supply of a country is much larger than the base money created by the country's Central Bank. Anyway, public authorities still have control over monetary decisions by means of regulating the base money, the interest rate and the reserve and other financial ratio requirements to private banks. We shall see the fractional-reserve banking system and the role played by Central Banks more in detail[15], but for now let us continue with further historical insight.

1.4. How Other Financial Markets Appeared

During the 12th and 13th centuries, in France, Flanders and Venetia people started trading with commodities and government securities. Those were the precedents of the stock markets as we know them today. The age of discovery, during the 16th century, was crucial to the development of a new type of enterprise: joint stock companies of limited liability, capitalist societies through which investors financed business ventures to the newfound lands. In 1602, the Dutch East India Company *(Verenigde Oost-Indische Compagnie)* was the first company to issue stocks and bonds[16] to be traded at the Bourse of Amsterdam, considered since then the oldest Stock Exchange in the world.

Through the years, financial markets have evolved each step to a greater degree of complexity. On financial venues bonds and stocks, currencies and commodities have been traded for centuries. The last decades of the 20th century have also witnessed the development of the derivatives markets, which in turn have their origins in Chicago, 19th century, as we shall see in the derivatives section[17]. Promoting a consistent and smooth real economic growth, improving liquidity of the economy and matching risk requirements of hedgers and speculators have been the forces behind the development of the financial markets, which we shall see next in more detail.

Beurse van Berlage. Amsterdam Municipal Department for the Preservation and Restoration of Historic Buildings and Sites (bMA).

[15] See chapter 2 below.

[16] Stocks and bonds, among other financial assets, shall be defined and described in chapters 4 and 3, respectively.

[17] See section 5.2 below.

1.5. Financial Markets or the Essence of the Economy

Nowadays financial markets can be classified in some different ways. We will follow as the most significant those proposed by Blake (2000), namely physical vs. over-the-counter markets, continuous vs. call markets, money vs. capital markets, and primary vs. secondary markets. Next, we briefly explain the main features of each one of these markets.

Four alternative ways to classify financial markets:

- Physical vs. OTC markets
- Continuous vs. call markets
- Money vs. capital markets
- Primary vs. secondary markets

Physical vs. over-the-Counter (OTC) Markets

By physical or exchange markets we mean all transactions that take place in the registered stock exchanges around the world. Formerly, those transactions were carried out by agents (brokers, dealers, and so on) trading on the market floor. Today most of the negotiation is not traded physically but electronically through computer networks. Still, we consider physical markets as those registered exchanges in which listed securities are traded through continuous auction, only members can trade and the broker acts as an intermediary between the buyer and the seller.

For a security to be traded on an exchange market it has to be listed there. Most equity stocks are traded through exchange markets. Examples are those better known by the public: the New York Stock Exchange (NYSE), the London Stock Exchange (LSE) or the stock exchanges at Frankfurt, Tokyo, Paris, Zurich, Milan, Madrid, etc. The International Federation of Stock Exchanges includes sixty nine exchanges in more than forty countries[18].

On the other hand, OTC markets include the trading in all securities not listed on any of the registered exchanges. If a dealer is willing to make a market in a specific security, it can be traded in these negotiated markets where investors trade directly with the dealers instead of through continuous auction markets in which brokers intermediate between buyers and sellers as it happens with registered exchanges.

One can figure out the dimension of this market considering that U.S. OTC market is the largest in terms of number of issues traded, that in terms of value it negotiates a volume similar to the NYSE, and that most of bond trading takes place in OTC operations. The best known OTC market was the National Association of Securities Dealers Automated Quotation (NASDAQ) until it converted to an official regulated market in 1987. Stocks listed on a registered exchange may also be traded over-the-counter: non-member investment firms can trade registered securities without going through the exchange. This segment is called the 'Third Market', as we will see later.

[18] See <www.world-exchanges.org/>.

Four alternative ways to classify financial markets:

- Physical vs. OTC markets
- Continuous vs. call markets
- Money vs. capital markets
- Primary vs. secondary markets

Continuous vs. Call Markets

In most markets, trades can take place at any time the market is open. The price is continuously set by the auction process or by dealer bid-ask quotes: bids (the prices at which agents are willing to buy a security) and asks or offers (the prices at which agents owning the security are willing to sell it) are faced, and a new price for the security is set every time a buyer accepts to pay the lowest ask price, or a seller accepts to sell the security at the highest bid price available.

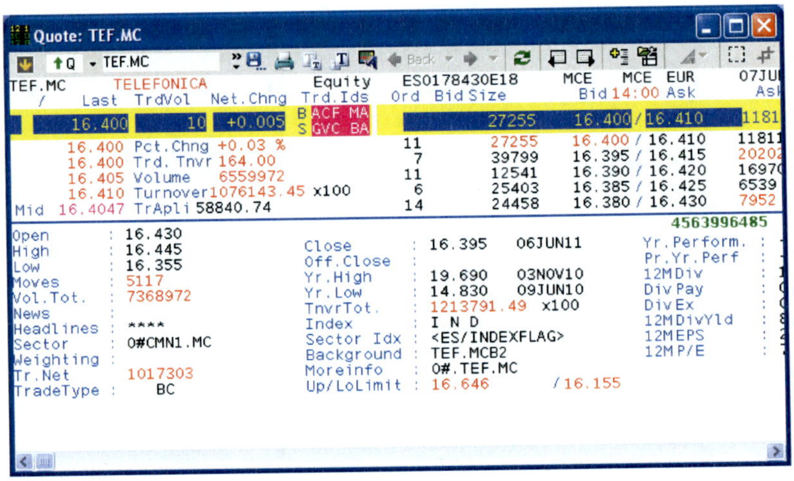

Source: Reuters.

Figure 1. Bid - ask quotes on a trading screen.

We can see in figure 1 above how bid and ask prices are quoted in a common trading screen. Market makers (called specialists in U.S., and Saitori in Japan) have the responsibility of keeping an orderly market, providing continuous buy and sell prices in all market conditions. Orders sent to the system may be market orders, to buy or sell at the best price available and which therefore generate necessarily a transaction, and limit orders, to buy or sell away from the current market price and which provide the market with liquidity. Liquidity demanders place market orders, and liquidity suppliers place limit orders. The difference between the highest bid price and the lowest ask price at any time is known as the bid-ask spread: its size is a measure of the liquidity of the market and the size of the transaction cost, since it measures the cost of making transactions without delay.

In contrast, call markets are those where stocks are traded only at specific times, and where the bid and ask orders are aggregated and transacted at once. Such markets are named so because securities are 'called' for trading: all trades, bids and asks, are declared, and then one negotiated price is set that clears the market for the stock. This method is used in smaller markets, and to set the opening price in major markets too. Some financial futures and options, and certain precious metals such as gold are also usually traded through call markets.

Money vs. Capital Markets

> **Four alternative ways to classify financial markets:**
>
> - Physical vs. OTC markets
> - Continuous vs. call markets
> - Money vs. capital markets
> - Primary vs. secondary markets

According to the maturity of the securities traded, financial markets can be classified between money markets, where securities with less than one year to maturity are traded, and capital markets, for those with more than one year. This classification gives us little information about how financial markets actually work, but it is probably the most commonly used to differentiate markets according to the type of assets that are traded.

In money markets, money and other liquid assets can be lent and borrowed for between a few hours and a few months. Government securities with less than one year to maturity when issued (like Treasury bills in the U.S.), bonds with less than one year to maturity and repurchase agreements ('repo'), among other securities, would be included in this category. For private securities, the list includes commercial paper, certificates of deposit, bankers' acceptances or short-lived mortgage-backed and asset-backed securities, among others.

Capital markets, on the other hand, cover both debt and equity markets. Regarding debt markets these include instruments such as government bonds with more than a year to maturity and many different types of corporate debt. In turn, equity markets include all shares traded at stock markets.

Finally, as financial markets have gained in complexity, we should consider as well other markets not included above under this classification: the derivatives markets, foreign exchange markets and other alternative investments like real estate, commodities or private equity.

Primary vs. Secondary Markets

> **Four alternative ways to classify financial markets:**
>
> - Physical vs. OTC markets
> - Continuous vs. call markets
> - Money vs. capital markets
> - Primary vs. secondary markets

In the primary markets, new bonds and stocks are issued for the first time. When a government wants to sell new bills and bonds, or when a company already trading at the stock market wants to issue new shares, they must do it through primary markets. Most issues are distributed with the aid of an underwriter (generally an investment bank), which provides three services: origination (involving design, planning and security registration), risk bearing (if the investment firm guarantees the price by purchasing the assets) and distribution (selling the issue to the customers).

Government bonds are sold at public auctions with either competitive or non-competitive bids. Other private and public bond issues can also include a negotiated underwriting, where the underwriter bears the price risk and distribute the asset for a negotiated fee, and private placements, where governments or private agents sell the issue directly to investors without the help of an underwriter. Corporate stock issues are generally sold with the assistance of an investment bank, and involve either seasoned issues (companies already trading in the market issuing new shares) and initial public offerings (IPOs) or first time issues by firms not negotiated yet.

What about secondary markets? They are venues where securities are traded after they have been issued on primary markets. Their fundamental role is to provide investors with liquidity for their investments and with continuous information about the market price of their securities. For a firm trying to raise new capital, having its shares already trading at a secondary market makes it easier to find investors willing to buy the new shares. Continuous information about the price at which old shares are being traded reduces the risk of mispricing the new ones from the investor's point of view. Furthermore, once the new shares are bought, they know they have a market where they can sell the new shares at any time, which reduces their liquidity risk[19]. These improvements are essential to understand how secondary markets, especially at the stock exchanges, have contributed to an extraordinary development of financial markets around the world and their importance in the capitalist economies today.

Finally, under this classification we should consider as well the third and fourth markets. The third market simply refers to the fact that securities listed on a registered exchange can also be traded in OTC markets. These trades allow institutional investors to trade blocks of securities directly, providing liquidity to sellers and anonymity to buyers. Likewise, the fourth market describes the direct exchange of securities between investors without the services of a broker. Needless to say that direct sales allow saving transaction costs and are not subject to reporting requirements.

For the purposes of this book, we are going to study the variety of financial markets there exist in terms of which assets are traded on them. The most common classification is that which distinguishes between money markets, which provide agents with means of payment, and capital markets, where they get their long-term financing, either external (debt markets) or self financing (equities). And apart from them, agents can operate internationally, hedge risks, speculate or invest in non-financial assets through foreign exchange, derivatives and alternative markets.

This way, we distinguish six basic groups of financial markets: Money markets, debt markets, equity markets, foreign exchange markets, derivatives markets, and alternative investments markets. We shall see each one of them in detail through chapters 2 to 5 of this part of the book.

---

[19] See the definition of liquidity risk in section 3.4.

Chapter 2

MONEY MARKETS

As in the Bank of England's early days, modern financial institutions in charge of a country's monetary policy, such as the Fed or the ECB, are responsible for maintaining money supply in a level that promotes growth of wealth and price stability within an economy. But whereas in the past increasing (or decreasing) money supply was as simple as just printing more banknotes and issuing more coins (or either withdraw them from circulation), in present days things are much more complex than that.

The four functions of money:

- Medium of exchange
- Store of value
- Unit of account
- Standard of deferred payment

In order to regulate the quantity of money circulating in the economy, economic authorities must consider all different expressions of money in financial markets. As above-mentioned, money is anything that is generally accepted as a payment for goods and services and for repayment of debts, meeting the four main functions necessary for that: medium of exchange, store of value, unit of account and standard of deferred payment.

First, as a medium of exchange, money must be useful in trading to avoid the inconveniences of barter—coincidence of both goods and/or services at the market at the same time and for traders willing to exchange them—as we have seen before. Second, as a store of value, it must be a storable good that can be saved and used to transfer purchasing power into the future, and retrieved at any time. Related to this function of money are the essential financial concepts of liquidity (the degree to which an asset can be bought or sold in the market without a significant movement in its price) and inflation (the overall increase in the level of prices of goods and services within an economy). Third, as a unit of account, money has to allow apples and milk can be added in some common value. This is because all goods, services and assets can be given a price by measuring them in comparison with a standard unit. Under conditions of price stability, money as a unit of account improves the efficiency of market economies since it allows agents taking their saving, spending, trading and investment decisions within a framework of stable information. Therefore, it is the primary objective of monetary authorities to combat the effects that inflation and deflation have on the stability of money as a unit of account. Finally, a standard of deferred payment is also sometimes mentioned as the fourth function of money, although it actually represents a combination of the second and the third properties when used over time. It means money serves not only as a measure of value today, but also as a standard for future payments to settle a debt.

Given that definition, it is essential to understand that there is further much money in our economies that meet all those four functions than just the banknotes and coins in circulation. We are going to see that by explaining first how money is issued in our economies today, how money supply is broken down into several categories and which assets are traded today in money markets.

2.1. Fractional-Reserve Banking System

In modern economies, more than 90% of money is not created directly by the State, but by private agents. Governments have ceded their right of seignorage to private banks. Why? As we have seen before, they realized printing money only generates inflation, so the banking system has been empowered with the right to create new money.

How do private banks create money? Under a fractional-reserve banking system, they keep only a fraction of their clients' deposits tied up in reserves, while the remainder is lent to other costumers through credit operations. This situation where at least two different people 'own' the same piece of money (the client that maintains her deposit under the bank's compromise to redeem it upon demand, and the costumer that receives that amount in credit) actually expands money supply. We will see it clearer through an example.

Example 1

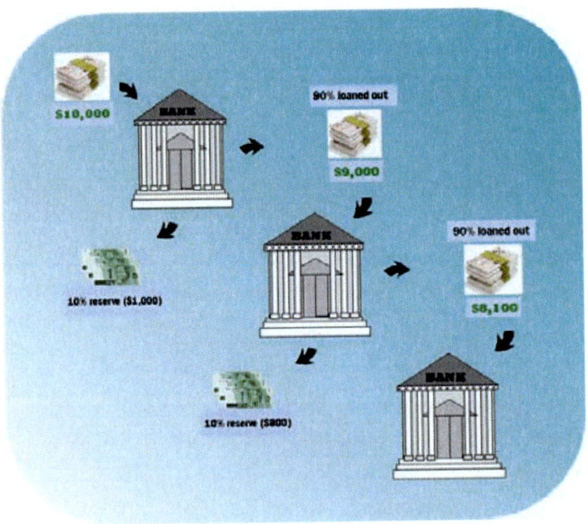

Julia goes to a bank and deposits an amount of money there, say $10,000. She receives a return for it there, and it can be withdrawn at any time at first call, so she knows her money is safely stored. Right after she leaves the bank office, John, a second client willing to buy a new car, is granted a loan of $10,000. One may think of those $10,000 as the same as those deposited by Julia. In fact, it could happen that the same banknotes and coins had been used in both transactions, so one could think of it as John leaving the bank with Julia's money.

That morning John visits a car dealer and buys his brand new car paying with cash. The car dealer has some payments to make to a supplier, but prefers not to spend cash so she pays with an IOU note, a promissory note. In some way she is paying with $10,000 Julia deposited in the bank, but actually keeping that amount in her cash account! Her supplier goes to another bank office and asks to be paid that amount in advance. He goes shopping, but instead of paying with cash he uses his credit card... and the wheel keeps on rolling.

Obviously, banks do not grant loans for all money in their deposits. Central banks mandate reserve requirements that oblige them to keep a minimum fraction of their deposits in reserves, so here is where the name fractional-reserve banking comes from. Under this system, reserves are used to meet normal demand for withdrawals, with central banks acting as a lender of last resort to avoid a bank run, in case an abnormal number of costumers trying to cash their deposits exceeds its reserves.

Fractional-reserve banking expands money supply in the economy far beyond the base money created by financial authorities. The number of times the money supply exceeds the currency (notes and coins) in circulation is called money multiplier, and is determined by the reserve requirement. Technically, the money multiplier m is measured as

$$m = 1 / R, \qquad (2)$$

where R represents the reserve requirement the central banks impose to the private banking sector.

Example 1 (Continued)

Given a reserve requirement of R = 10%, in our example before it would imply that the \$10,000 deposited by Julia will generate \$100,000 (\$10,000/0.1 = \$100,000) of total money supply, at most, depending on economic conditions. Some readers may find this example unrealistic; they would be surprised then, when we see later in this section that the currency in circulation for the euro or the U.S. dollar represents less than the 10% of the total money supply in those economies.

Of the three possible banking systems (fractional-reserve, full-reserve and free banking), the first one[1] is considered to be the most efficient because it allows the supply of money to adjust to changes in its demand. On the contrary, a full-reserve banking system would imply banks can not grant loans and people are not allowed to borrow, which is nonsense somewhat, and imply a fixed money supply that can result in deflation as the economy grows. Finally, under free banking, where banks are not subject to any constraints regarding reserve requirements, economic authorities would lose control over the supply of money, and there would be no role for central bank: there would be no lender of last resort, no insurance for deposit accounts, and no way for economic authorities to execute monetary policies.

At the end of this section, and as an aside, we will learn more about the banking system, the reasons why financial intermediaries exist, and the functions they conduct today in market economies, in 'Microeconomics of banking'. Now we are going to continue our tour through money markets taking a view on assets and participants involved.

[1] In fact, fractional-reserve banking system was a consequence of bank lending, since they should have cash reserves enough to meet their depositor's withdrawals.

2.2. Money Supply

Money supply in an economy is the total amount of money—in its several forms—available at any time. Due to the close relation that money supply, economic growth and inflation rate have shown empirically over time, it is the primary concern for policy makers to control it through monetary policies.

One difficulty for monetary authorities is how to measure the relevant money supply aggregate. There are several different methods, reflecting the different degree of liquidity of various sorts of money. For analytic purposes, money supply is broken down into several different types of assets based on the effect monetary policies can have on them. Money aggregates consider narrow measures that include those assets more directly affected by monetary policy, as well as broader measures for those less influenced by economic authority actions. This is generally described with a set of measures, ranging from M0 (the narrowest) to M3[2] (the broadest). The M0 aggregate includes only cash (notes and coins) in circulation or in bank vaults. When bank reserves at the Central Bank are included, such a measure would consider all Monetary Base within an economy, so it is usually referred as MB. It is the most liquid and the narrowest measure of money, since it considers all money issued by the Central Bank and can be directly controlled by it.

On the other hand, non-MB components of money supply are commercial bank money derived from the practice of fractional-reserve banking. The aggregate M1 is known as narrow money and consists mainly of physical currency in circulation plus the most liquid types of commercial bank money, such as current account deposits, traveller's checks or other checkable deposits (OCDs). Anyway, these 'Ms' measures depend as well on which definition we are using. For example, for euro currency[3] it is considered as M1 only the cash in circulation plus overnight deposits.

The M2 aggregate represents money and 'close substitutes' for it, and it is the widest used indicator to monitor money supply and to forecast inflation for a country or an economic area[4]. It includes M1 plus savings deposits redeemable at a period of notice up to three months, time deposits with an agreed maturity up to two years, money market accounts and retail money market mutual funds. Finally, M3 is the broadest measure of money supply and includes all money within an economy. This aggregate is formed by all assets included in M2 measure plus large time deposits, short-term repurchase agreements, institutional money market funds and all types of debt securities with maturities up to two years.

Example 2

We may see money aggregates both for U.S. and Eurozone economies in figure 2.

The main purpose of showing the data above is to make our readers understand that most of the money circulating in any economy is 'private money', not directly issued by financial authorities. In most markets, MB has historically represented less than 10% of all money

[2] M4 in the U.K.

[3] The ECB's definition of money aggregates is at <http://www.ecb.int/stats/money/aggregates/aggr/html/hist.en.html>.

[4] In fact, the M2/M0 ratio is considered an empirical measure of the so-called money multiplier.

assets in the economy, and the last two decades this ratio has been even lower. In the U.S. economy, for example, physical coins and paper money represented in January 2010 only 10.1% of M2 measure[5], and this ratio could possibly be lower than 5% when compared against the total money supply (M3), although we do not have an official measure since the Fed does not release data on M3 since year 2006. Things in the Eurozone[6] were not very different: in January 2010 total amount of coins (21.16 billion euros) and banknotes (783.5 billion euros) represented 8.6% of the broadest measure, M3.

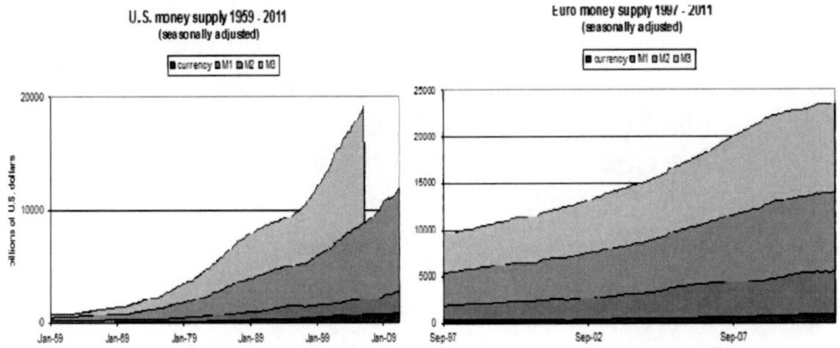

Source: <www.federalreserve.gov> and www.ecb.int.

Figure 2. U.S. and Eurozone money supply.

All other types of money outside the monetary base are privately issued, represent more than 90% of money assets in circulation, and are not directly under the control of Central Banks. Hence, considering this fact the key point is: how does monetary authority regulate money supply for monetary policy and price control purposes? We address this question in the next section.

2.3. How Central Banks Regulate Money Aggregates in the Economy

Three are the basic instruments Central Banks have to implement their monetary policy: controlling the level of interest rates, mandating reserve requirements to private banks, and executing open market operations. Next we examine each one in detail.

Instruments of monetary policy:

- Interest rates
- Reserve requirements
- Open market operations

Interest Rates

An interest rate is the price one agent must pay for using money during a specific period of time. As in any other market, there are both a supply and a demand for money: households, companies and institutions willing to lend their savings face agents willing to borrow them. Demand and

[5] See <http://www.federalreserve.gov/releases/h6/Current/>.
[6] For ECB statistics see <http://www.ecb.int/stats/services/downloads/html/index.en.html>.

supply for money then determine the price the latter will pay the former for using money, and that price is called the interest rate.

Anyway, there is one market where price for money is not determined only by supply and demand: the one where the Central Bank regulates the liquidity of the economy through money auctions to private banks. Central Banks settle an official set of interest rates at which either they lend or borrow money to private banks. In the Eurozone, for example, three interest rates are set. The refinancing rate is the minimum interest rate at which, in open market operations, private banks compete for liquidity at Central Bank's auctions. On the other hand, the marginal lending facility rate, also known as the discount rate, is the interest rate the ECB charges depository institutions that need to borrow reserves from it. In the Eurozone the ECB usually sets this rate one hundred basis points (1%) above the refinancing rate. Finally, the deposit facility rate is the rate the ECB is willing to pay for deposits placed by private banks in their reserve accounts at the central bank. It is usually set one hundred basis points below the refinancing rate.

The refinancing rate is the reference rate for monetary operations, and it constitutes the most important tool financial authorities have to implement their policies. Through it, Central Banks try both to influence private banks' credit decisions and hence to regulate money supply in order to maintain inflation under control. Whenever a bank wants to refinance short term, it may do so by attending the ECB's weekly refinancing operations, paying interest on money they borrow. If the interest rate is quite high, the bank will restrict credit to their costumers knowing the refinancing of those funds will be expensive; the opposite behaviour will take place when the bank considers the interest rate low enough.

We may see in figure 3 that financial authorities (here, the Fed and the ECB) have been very active raising and falling interest rates to pursue their macroeconomic objectives.

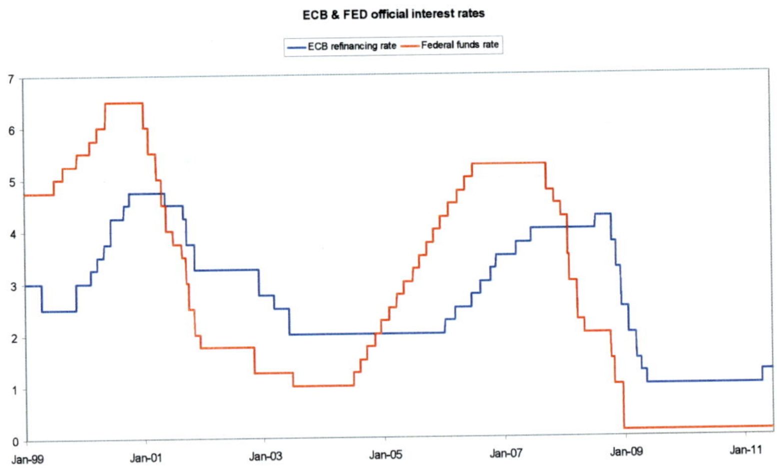

Source: <www.ecb.int> and www.federalreserve.gov.

Figure 3. Official set of interest rates in the Eurozone and the U.S. since 1999.

In the U.S. the process described above is regulated through the Federal funds rate, that is, the interest rate at which private banks lend their balances at the Fed to other depository institutions, usually overnight. The weighted average of this rate across all transactions is the

Federal funds effective rate. Instead of setting a minimum refinancing rate as the ECB does, the Fed determines its 'Federal funds target rate', and executes open market operations to make that Federal funds effective rate follow its target.

A discount rate—the rate depository institutions are charged for borrowing reserves from the Fed—is also set. Although the Federal funds rate is determined by the supply and demand for funds of private banks borrowing and lending to each other, the Fed has unlimited capacity to influence this rate, and in practice it generally stays within a limited range above and below the target set by the authorities.

One problem reference rates exhibit as a monetary policy tool is the 'zero lower bound' problem: interest rates are constrained by the fact that, under a scenario of economic depression and low inflation (or even deflation), setting the nominal interest rate below 0% would be ineffective, because economic agents would prefer to hold their assets in cash rather than to invest them at a negative rate. This is a serious problem that constrains Central Banks ability to fight against severe recessions, as it happened to Japan during the 1990s and could perhaps happen today to most advanced economies. Under that situation the economy would fall into what is known as a (Keynesian) liquidity trap[7], where monetary policies become ineffective to boost aggregate demand. Recent works by Buiter (2009), Mankiw (2009) and Shastri (2010), among others, have proposed several procedures to avoid this situation, which basically would require abolish physical currency or impose taxes on currency holdings otherwise.

Instruments of monetary policy:

- Interest rates
- <u>Reserve requirements</u>
- Open market operations

Reserve Requirements

The second tool in hands of Central Banks to regulate money supply in the economy consists of the reserve requirements they impose to private banks. As we have mentioned before, banks must never lent a minimum amount of their costumers' deposits. Those reserves can adopt the form of currency in bank vaults, or electronic records in reserve accounts at the Central Bank. Reserve ratio, that is, the minimum proportion of funds banks can never lend, is determined by the Central Bank. Since the money multiplier (the maximum amount of commercial bank money that can be created per unit of monetary base directly issued by public authorities) is inversely related to the reserve ratio[8], Central Banks can have some control over the M1-M3 measures of money aggregates by either increasing or decreasing the reserve requirements.

In practice, since private banks can accumulate excess reserves, it is quite tough for economic authorities to regulate the money supply through the reserve requirements, because a mandate to increase them can be followed by a decision of the private bank to reduce its (voluntary) excess reserves, offsetting their effects. Hence, Central Banks prefer to use open market operations for monetary policy purposes.

---

[7] A 'liquidity trap' occurs as interest rates approach the zero lower bound and the demand for money becomes infinitely elastic (that is, horizontal when drawn against the interest rate), so further increases of money in the economy would fail to reduce interest rates. For further details, see Krugman (2000).

[8] Remember equation (2).

Instruments of monetary policy:

- Interest rates
- Reserve requirements
- Open market operations

Open Market Operations

Through open market operations, Central Banks regulate the stock of money in a economy by buying and selling financial assets at money markets. Whenever a Central Bank buys a security in exchange for money, it increases money supply; on the contrary, when it sells an asset in its balance, money is drained and its supply reduced.

A Central Bank can better execute its monetary policy this way. Since most money is electronic, this process does not require immediate printing of new currency. Rather, it simply increases or decreases the amount of money a private bank has in its reserve account at the Central Bank. Only when the private bank demands banknotes, the authorities will print currency in exchange for a decrease in such electronic balance. As we have already seen, in the U.S. the Fed sets a federal interest target rate for overnight bank reserves, and makes open market operations to follow that target. For this purpose, the American authorities usually use an overnight repurchase agreement (also known as *repo*) to temporarily create or destroy (through 'reverse repos') money. In the Eurozone, on the other hand, the ECB sets a minimum interest rate for refinancing operations that apply to those repurchase agreements.

Although open market operations are the best tool Central Banks have to regulate money supply, they are not infallible. Effectiveness to control commercial bank money supply through Central Bank money creation in open market operations directly depends on the level of excess reserves commercial banks maintain. If they have low excess reserves, broad money supply is easy to be monitored. But when commercial banks accumulate excess reserves well above the mandated reserve requirements—as it happens during a financial crisis—it is more difficult for Central Banks to make private banks increase their money supply than to make it shrink.

This asymmetry of monetary policy is known as a *pushing on a string* situation, meaning it is easier for Central Banks to smooth an economic expansion than to end a recession. When the economic activity is growing faster than the authorities wish, market operations are implemented to reduce monetary base, so private banks are *pulled* to cut lending, reducing commercial bank money (the broader aggregates of money supply). However, when the economy is facing a severe recession, most banks tend to accumulate excess reserves, and increases in central bank money may not result in an increase of the money supply, because banks are not *pushed* to lend it.

2.4. Money Markets: Public and Private Money Securities

After we have seen what money is, which aggregates are included in it, how money is created both by the Central Bank and the fractional-reserve banking system, and which policies can monetary authorities execute to have money supply under control, we are ready to have an insight on what money markets are and which securities are traded in them.

A money market is a financial market where assets with short-term maturities are traded. Although there is no generally accepted definition for which short-term should it be for an asset to be included in money markets, all transactions from overnight to a one-year period are included, and some authors consider as well securities with maturities up to two years maximum. Most money market operations are actually no other thing than electronic transactions among central banks and depository institutions, borrowing and lending one to each other. Therefore, money markets are sometimes referred as the interbank market.

Banks market those borrowings and lendings with financial securities commonly known as 'paper'. A paper is priced to 'yield' a determined interest rate, that depends on which currency the paper is denominated, its maturity term and the set of reference interest rates that is generally used to price such kind of securities. The most commonly used set of reference rates, both in E.U. and U.S., for benchmarking money market operations are the London Interbank Offered Rate (Libor), the Euro Interbank Offered Rate (Euribor), the U.S. Federal Funds rate (FFR), and the Euro Overnight Index Average (Eonia).

Libor is the most important set of reference rates worldwide, determined at the London interbank market. Released everyday by the British Bankers' Association, it represents

> the benchmark used by banks, securities houses and investors to gauge the cost of unsecured borrowing in the money markets. It is calculated each day by asking a panel of major banks what it would cost them to borrow funds for various periods of time and in various currencies, and then creating an average[9],

called Libor for such specific currency and period of time. It is produced for ten currencies with 15 maturities quoted for each, ranging from overnight to 12 months, through quotes from a panel of at least eight contributor banks for each currency calculated. Libor provides a benchmark for pricing many different types of financial instruments such as mortgage agreements and loans, futures and options contracts (short-term interest rate futures contracts, FRAs, interest rate swaps...)[10], currencies, etc. Libor is considered to be the most important of all benchmarks for short-term interest rates globally, since it is generally accepted as the basis for settlement of most sterling and U.S. dollar denominated instruments, and for interest rate contracts in U.K., the Commonwealth, the U.S., non-Eurozone countries of the E.U., Switzerland, Japan, etc.

With the first issuance of the Euro currency in 1999, a new financial market has emerged with the integration of the economies of the sixteen E.U. countries that, so far, have adopted it. Since then, a new set of reference rates have been used as the main benchmark for money and capital markets in the Eurozone: the Euribor. Sponsored by the European Banking Federation, Euribor

> is the rate at which Euro interbank term deposits are being offered by one prime bank to another within the EMU zone11.

Quotes are currently contributed from a panel of 43 major banks worldwide, most of them from E.U. countries in the Eurozone, but banks from non-Eurozone countries and large international banks from non-E.U. countries, both with important Eurozone operations, are also considered[12]. That set of reference rates is the main benchmark for Euro-denominated

[9] The bbalibor definition can be found at <http://www.bbalibor.com>.
[10] We shall describe most of them in section 5.2.
[11] The Euribor definition can be found at <http://www.euribor.org/>.
[12] Non-Eurozone contributors include, among others, Barclays Capital, Citibank, J.P. Morgan Chase & Co. or UBS.

money market instruments, depending on their maturity. For such purpose, an Euribor rate is released every market day for maturities of one, two and three weeks, and of one to twelve months. In figure 4 the recent evolution of 12-month Euribor rate is depicted.

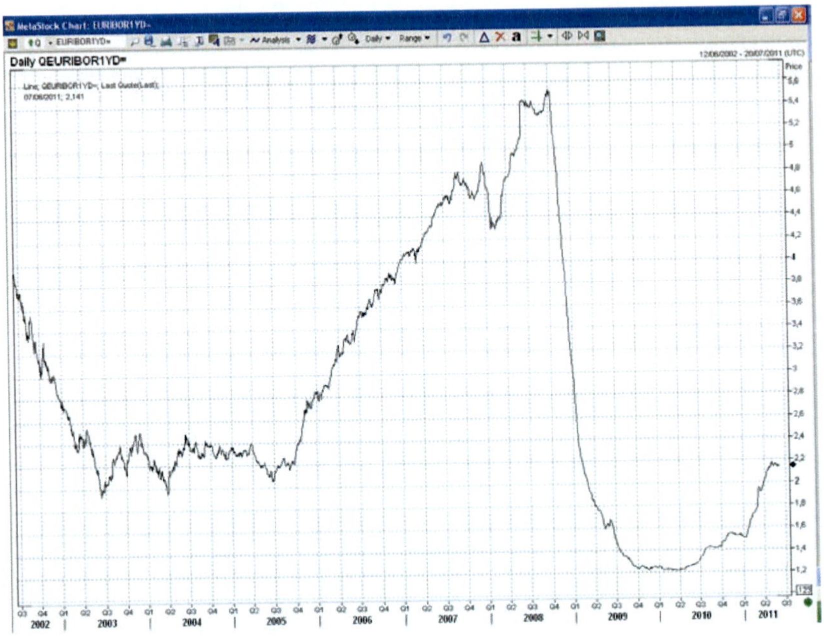

Source: MetaStock.

Figure 4. 12-month Euribor rate.

Lastly, for overnight operations—meaning transactions to be delivered from today to tomorrow—another two commonly used reference rates are released: the FFR in the U.S., and the Eonia in E.U. While the FFR, as we have already seen, is the rate at which private depository institutions lend overnight their balances at the Fed to other banks, the Eonia reference rate is calculated by the ECB using data from the same panel banks quoting for Euribor. Both FFR and Eonia are the two most important reference rates at the interbank markets for the U.S. dollar and Eurozone, respectively. All reference rates above are always expressed on an equivalent annual basis, no matter the maturity term they are referred. This allows for comparison of interest rates among different periods[13].

Money market securities can be issued by both private and public institutions. Public securities such as Treasury bills and deposits issued by the banking sector represent the bulk of the assets in the money markets, but the list is more extensive. Apart from that classification, we consider two main classes of money market securities: those that are quoted on a yield basis and those quoted on a discount basis[14].

[13] It is important to notice that while in U.K. money market a 365-day year is used to calculate interest payments, both in the U.S. and the Eurozone a 360-day year is assumed. These methods are known respectively as actual/365 and actual/360. Since money market instruments provide a return for every day between payments, under the actual/360 method a one-year money market instrument accrues an interest rate of 365/360 times its nominal interest rate.

[14] See Blake (2000).

MM securities quoted on a yield basis:

- MMDs
- CDs

Securities quoted on a yield basis are always issued at par, meaning the price paid at the release of the instrument equals the nominal value of that financial security. Return on those instruments come from the interest paid on capital, usually in one lump sum on the maturity day. Money market deposit accounts (MMDs) are fixed-interest fixed-term savings accounts of up to one year. They are generally not negotiable so cannot be liquidated before maturity. At a given date, capital is deposited with the interest and maturity fixed in advance. On maturity date, interest and capital are paid in one lump sum, where the interest is calculated according to the following formula for simple interest

$$I = N \cdot r \cdot \frac{n}{360}, \quad (3)$$

where I is the total interest, N the face value of the deposit, r the interest rate on deposit and n the number of days between deposit and maturity dates. Negotiable certificates of deposit (CDs), besides, are receipts from banks for deposits that have been made with them. They can be traded in secondary markets, so we can think of CDs as negotiable MMDs.

MM securities quoted on a discount basis:

i) Public securities

- Treasury bills

ii) Private securities

- Commercial bills
- Banker's acceptances
- Commercial paper
- Note issuance facilities

On the other hand, securities quoted on a discount basis are sold at issuance for a price below its nominal value. Return on those instruments comes from the difference between the price paid and the face value received in return at the maturity date. Several securities can be mention in this case. Public securities—Treasury bills both in the U.S. and the U.K.—are short-term government promissory notes where at maturity (usually three, six and sometimes twelve months after being issued) the holder receives the par value of the bill. They are said to be pure discount securities because they pay no explicit interest, that is, the holder receives just the return from buying it at a discount.

Privately issued securities include a vast and growing list The most common are *commercial bills*, similar to Treasury bills but issued by private companies against the sale of goods; *banker's acceptances*, or written promises issued by borrowers to banks to repay borrowed funds; *commercial paper*, unsecured promissory notes issued by large corporations that are not backed by any collateral, they only rely on the credit rating of the issuing corporation; and *note issuance facilities*, a commitment between a borrowing company and a bank, whereby the former can issue commercial paper in its own name, though the issue is effectively underwritten by the latter: examples include euronotes, eurocommercial paper, multiple component facility, revolving underwriting facilities, etc.

Finally, we should not forget three other important actors on money markets: debt securities with a short term to maturity, transactions on interest rate derivatives, and investments in money market securities. Debt securities with a short term to maturity are issued on capital markets as long-term investments, but after some time they can be considered as money market securities when they are traded on markets whenever their period to maturity is below 12-24 months. On the other hand, many transactions in money markets are settled through interest rate derivatives, such as FRAs, interest rate swaps, etc. We shall see them on the derivatives section of this book. Finally, money market funds are regulated investment companies—like other mutual funds—that invest in money market securities. They compete as a vehicle for investment with savings deposits, although they cannot be formally considered as money market securities.

2.5. Aside: Microeconomics of Banking[15]

As we saw in section 1.2, banks appeared at the same time financial markets emerged. In most markets, and theoretically, under the Arrow-Debreu general equilibrium model[16], there is no necessity for intermediaries to exist in order to achieve a set of prices such that demand and supply for that market are aligned. Hence, one issue that has always worried economists when trying to explain how financial markets work is why do financial intermediaries exist? The existence of not just the banking sector, but of brokers and dealers, mutual funds, insurance companies and financial intermediaries other than these must be explained. We will offer the answer while we understand what do banks do, that is, which kind of activities they undertake.

A first justification for the presence of banks in the economy is the existence of transaction costs. In such way, banks can be seen as simply retailers of financial securities: they buy the securities issued by borrowers (granting loans) and sell them to lenders (collecting deposits), the same way as a retailer buys goods or services from producers in order to sell them to final consumers. Under this argument, economies of scale appear.

A closer insight shows banking as a retail activity is more complex than that. Usually banks deal with financial contracts (such as loans and deposits) that are not easily marketable, so their job does not consist of a simple buy and sale trading activity. Further than that, the characteristics of securities issued by borrowers are usually different from those desired by investors. Therefore, banks, mutual funds and insurance companies exist to transform and adapt financial contracts and securities. This role will be essential for managing risks, too. Risks and effects of moral hazard[17] are also the reasons why financial intermediaries develop long term relationships with borrowers that allow them to establish monitoring activities that reduces risks.

Banking functions:

- Liquidity and payment services
- Asset transformation
- Risk management
- Information processing

Given all that, contemporary banking theory has classified banking functions into four categories: liquidity and payment services, asset transformation, risk management, and monitoring and information processing. Regarding liquidity and payment services, it would have no sense in a world without transaction costs, in which case commerce would be conducted through barter. But as money appeared, banks were born

[15] For a complete review on this issue, see Freixas and Rochet (1997).
[16] See Arrow and Debreu (1954).
[17] Moral hazard is any situation in which one person makes the decision about how much risk to take, while someone else bears the cost if things go badly. See Krugman (2009).

at the same with duties like providing money change, developing payment services, offer deposits to store money at their vaults, etc.

The asset transformation role played by banks emerges from the fact that they provide three types of security transformation. Firstly, convenience of denomination implies that the bank chooses the unit size of its products (deposits and loans) that are suitable for their clients. Secondly, maturity transformation provides the transformation of short time securities (deposits) into securities of longer maturities (loans) borrowers desire. Thirdly, quality transformation occurs when a bank sells a portfolio of loans, since their risk-return characteristics improve those of the individual investments.

On the other hand, that banks manage risk refers to the fact that they face several different sources of risk affecting financial markets. In particular, they must deal with credit risk, interest rate risk, liquidity risk and off-balance-sheet operational risks.

Finally, processing and monitoring of information is unavoidable for banks since they usually have imperfect information on borrowers that leads to moral hazard problems. What banks do to mitigate the effects of moral hazard is to establish long term relationships with their clients. Nevertheless, it can be noted that while the effects of information asymmetries on the borrowers' side have been extensively studied, the effects that moral hazard has on banks, on risk-adjusted valuation and on predatory lending[18] are yet to be analyzed.

[18] Effects which, by the way, we have clearly witnessed during the current financial crisis.

Chapter 3

DEBT MARKETS

As we have seen, according to the maturity of the securities traded in them, financial markets can be either money markets—for securities with less than one year to maturity—or capital markets—for those with more than one year. Money markets provide economic agents with means of payment and short-term liquidity, whereas capital markets provide financial resources to agents interested in engaging in long-term investments, resources that are lent by other market players with surplus savings available.

In capital markets long-term financial assets, either in form of debt or property, are traded. This distinction becomes essential: when talking about investments we distinguish fixed income securities from equity assets. So we also differentiate the markets where they are traded, debt and equity markets respectively. In debt markets we are considering only negotiable securities, since there are other non-marketable debt assets—bank loans, for example—which do not fall within our analysis. Fixed income securities represent a debt of the issuer, who remunerates the holder with the payment of an interest, either constant or not, until a specific maturity date. In equity markets, on the other hand, shares representing ownership stakes of the issuer are traded, and security holders receive dividends in return until an infinite or indeterminate maturity term. Both fields are so extensive that they require a separate study for a detailed analysis. We shall see equity markets on chapter 4, whereas the review of debt markets will be our main topic for the rest of this chapter.

3.1. FIXED INCOME SECURITIES

Fixed income securities represent a debt of the issuer (who is to borrow capital from the lender) with the holder of the title (the lender), generate a return not necessarily fixed but determined in advance, and have a maturity term that is normally set when issued. These assets represent a right for the holder to receive regular, fixed periodic payments during a period of time, and to receive back at the maturity date the amount borrowed by the issuer.

Figure 5 represents the issuing of a fixed income security. The issuer—which generally would be a public or private company—in need of financing, has the possibility of secure funding directly at capital markets. Since the capital needed is usually significant, in order to make it possible for any investor to buy a piece of debt, several bonds (of face value N, as in the figure) are sold. Each bond represents a quantity of N currency units that the lender delivers to the borrower when the bond is issued. In return, the bond gives the holder the right to receive several coupon payments on a regular basis, plus the right to receive the face value N back at the end of the life of the bond.

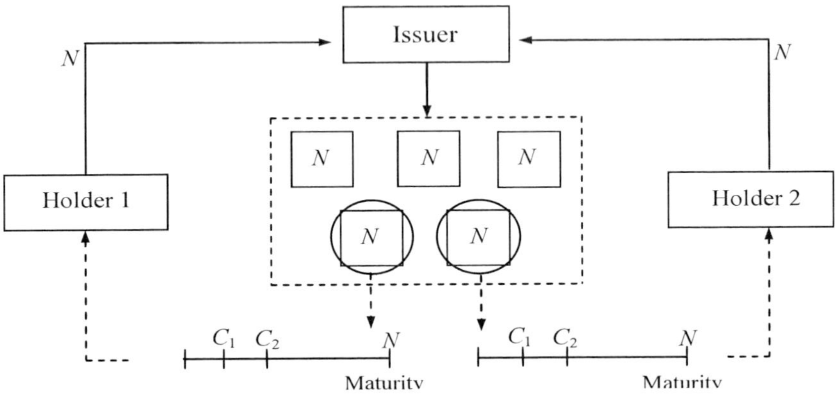

Figure 5. Issuing a fixed income security.

Several features are useful to describe debt securities. First, the entity, either public or private, that issues the asset for a specific value is called the issuer. According to that we differentiate public government bonds and private credit securities, and that will be the classification we shall use later on to analyze debt securities more in detail. The agent that buys the debt security, hence lending money to the issuer, is called the holder. The term to maturity—or simply, maturity—stands for the length of time until the loan contract expires, defining the life of the bond. It is determined by both the issuing and the expiration dates.

Return on bonds do not necessarily need to be constant, although they are considered to be 'fixed income' because, when issued, several properties (emission date, maturity term, interest rate, frequency of payments, etc.) are determined, and cannot be modified later on. These terms—known as covenants in the jargon—under which money is borrowed are contained in an agreement called indenture, and include both negative (prohibitions on the borrower) and affirmative (actions that the borrower promises to perform) sections. Anyway, fixed income securities accrue an interest that is generally fixed in advance. This way, the coupon rate is the one that, when multiplied by the par value of a bond, gives the amount of interest to be paid at every coupon payment date. Formally,

$$I = c \cdot N, \tag{4}$$

where I denotes the interest payment, c the coupon rate (in percentage) and N the face value of the bond. The amount of debt being recognized, i.e. the amount that the borrower promises to pay on or before the maturity date, receives several names: nominal, par or face value. On the other hand, the issuing price is the price being paid on the primary market when a security is sold. When nominal value and issuing price are equal, an asset is said to be issued at par.

The rating—or credit rating—represents the estimation of the credit worthiness of an agent, determined by the ability to repay its debts. Ratings are released by credit rating agencies, and are essential to assess the required return on securities, especially on those privately issued[1]. Right after their emission, bonds are exchanged at secondary markets and they are priced at any time a transaction occurs. Such price is called the quoted price. Market participants price debt securities considering their relevant features (maturity, rating, coupon rate, etc.) compared to other similar assets and interest rates being paid. We will show in section 3.4 below that there is an inverse relationship between interest rates on the market and the quoted price of a bond. This way, if market interest rates move above (below) the coupon rate of our bond, then it will sell below (above) its par value. A bond that trades above its par value is said to be trading at a premium, a bond that trades below its par value is trading at a discount. This essential relationship between the price of a bond and the interest rates on the market closely depends on the maturity term of the bond, as it will be explained later on under the key concept of duration.

There is a vast array of securities traded on debt markets. For a wider comprehension, we are going to describe them according to ten criteria; namely, their issuer, their holder, the maturity term, their issuing price, their redemption value, their coupon payments, their provisions for paying off the principal, their nationality, their guarantee, and their means of payment. They can be summarized as it follows.

Table 1. Taxonomy of fixed income assets

Issuer	Holder	Maturity term	Emission price	Redemption value
Coupon payment	Provisions for paying off the principal	Nationality	Guarantee	Means of payment

Issuer
- Government bonds
- Credit securities

Depending on the issuer, we distinguish between government bonds issued by the Treasury or local authorities, and credit securities issued by private agents.

Holder
- Nominative
- To bearer

According to their holder, fixed income assets can be nominative, where the holder is named, or to bearer, more frequently.

Maturity term
- Money Market securities
- Debt securities

Money market securities are fixed income assets with short-term maturities, generally below 12-18 months, whereas debt securities are those with maturity at the issuing time above 18 months. An alternative classification according to maturity allows us to distinguish amongst short-term, medium-term and long-term investments when duration (time to maturity) is up to three years, ten years and above ten years, respectively.

Emission price
- At par
- At a premium
- At a discount

On the other hand, assets are said to be issued at par, at a premium or at discount depending on whether they have been sold at the same price as the face value, above the nominal value, or below the nominal value, respectively.

[1] We shall describe ratings and credit rating agencies more in detail in section 3.3.

Redemption value
- At par
- At a premium
- Indexed
- With early amortization

And—do not get confused here—we can also talk about assets redeemed at par, when the holder receives the nominal value at the end of the investment, at a premium, when she receives a redemption premium, indexed, when the principal recovered depends on an index, such as the inflation rate, GDP growth, etc., or with early amortization provision, a type of credit enhancement used in asset backed securities, for example, where one or more triggers require the termination of contract.

Coupon payment
- Zero-coupon bonds
- Accrual bonds
- Fixed income bonds
- Floating rate securities
- Step-up notes
- Deferred coupon bonds

According to coupon payments we find zero-coupon bonds which make no coupon payments, but instead are sold at a deep discount from their par values. The difference between the initial price and the bond's par value at the end of the investment represents the interest earned. Accrual bonds are similar in a way to zero-coupon bonds since, although they do pay a stated interest every period, payments are deferred to maturity. However, unlike a zero-coupon bond, accrual bonds are issued at their par values and then appreciate from there.

Fixed income bonds, on the other hand, are those that pay regular fixed coupon payments according to their coupon rate and the face value of the asset, whereas floating rate securities pay a variable interest, in which case coupons depend on interest rate conditions pre-specified in the indenture. Floating rate securities consider the coupon formula given by

$$\text{Coupon rate} = \text{Reference rate} \pm \text{Spread}, \tag{5}$$

where usually the reference rate is the Libor or the Euribor. Floating rate notes (FRNs) fall under this category. In inverse floaters, however, coupon payments move inversely to the reference rate,

$$\text{Coupon rate} = k - m \cdot \text{Reference rate}, \tag{6}$$

where k is a constant and m is a multiplier. Other floating rate securities are dual-indexed floaters (with two reference rates to determine the coupon), range notes (the coupon rate is set equal to a reference rate within a pre-specified range, zero otherwise), index amortizing notes (with a structure for accelerated principal repayment before maturity) or non-interest rate indexed floaters (the coupon rate is not linked to any interest rate, but commonly to a commodity price). Step-up notes have coupon rates that increase over time at a pre-specified rate, so they could be considered both fixed rate and floating rate securities, in a way. Finally, deferred coupon bonds pay the first regular coupons after an initial deferment period.

Provisions for paying off the principal
- Bullet bonds
- Serial bonds
- Amortizing securities
- Sinking fund provisions
- Call provisions

How about provisions for paying off the principal? In this respect, bullet bonds pay the entire principal in one lump sum at maturity, whereas on serial bonds the principal is paid through a series of payments. Amortizing securities make periodic principal and interest payments, sinking fund provisions may require the retirement of a portion of a bond prior to maturity date and call provisions give issuers the right, but not the obligation, to retire all or a part of an issue prior to maturity. Such securities are called callable bonds, another form of embedded options we can find in fixed income securities.

Nationality
- National bonds
- Foreign bonds
- Eurobonds

Regarding their nationality, we may consider national bonds, foreign bonds and Eurobonds. National bonds are those issued by public or private agents of the same country as the holder. Hence, most securities are considered to be national. On the contrary, foreign bonds are issued in a country by institutions from another country[2], whereas Eurobonds are issued outside the legal system of any one country. They are offered simultaneously to investors in several countries, and are often registered on the Luxemburg, London or Zurich exchanges, though much of the Eurobond trading takes place in the OTC market.

Guarantee
- Debentures
- Mortgage-backed securities
- Asset-backed securities

According to the guarantee we distinguish debentures, MBS and ABS. Debentures are bonds where only the issuer's assets guarantee the investment. Mortgage-backed securities, MBS, represent a claim on the cash flows from a pool of mortgage loans that provide such assets as collateral. Finally, asset-backed securities, ABS, where the investment is backed by any specific asset[3], and bonds with the guarantee of third-parties, where a third party—usually a government—guarantees the investment.

Means of payment
- Regular bonds
- Convertible bonds
- Bonds with embedded options

Finally, according their means of payment there are regular bonds, where the principal is returned back in the form of money, convertible bonds, whenever the shares of the company will be redeem in return at the maturity of the bond[4], and bonds with embedded options, where the means and the timing of the payment is determined by the warrant[5].

From all those classifications above we are going to use the first one (public vs. private securities) to analyse fixed income securities more in detail. We will see it through the two following sections.

3.2. Government Bond Markets

Debt markets—also known as bond markets, credit markets or fixed income security markets—refer to those venues where debt securities are traded[6]. The main actors issuing debt

[2] Most common foreign bonds are *Yankee bonds* (traded in the U.S.), *Samurai bonds* (traded in Japan) or *Bulldog bonds* (traded in the U.K). Before the introduction of the Euro currency, foreign bonds such as *Rembrandt bonds* and *Matador bonds* were well known as well in the Netherlands and Spain, respectively.

[3] Mortgage-backed securities are no more than a specific type of asset-backed securities.

[4] Convertible bonds are usually issued together with a warrant, a derivative security traded separately that allows the holder to convert bonds into shares at an agreed-upon price. For more info, see warrants on the derivatives section.

[5] A warrant is a type of option derivatives we shall describe in section 5.2 below.

securities are governments. Public authorities, including federal, state and local administrations, finance their duties (social security, unemployment insurance, infrastructure, utilities and other facilities) with the taxes collected among the population. But usually that income is not sufficient to meet all expenses, so a budget deficit is generated that must be financed. For such purposes, governments issue national debt, i.e. a bunch of securities for different maturities that meets their funding needs, and providing investors with the possibility to obtain a safe return. We will get an insight on which government securities can be found on the markets by analyzing two different countries: the U.S. and Spain (as a country representative of the Eurozone, since U.E. does not issue—at least it does not yet—government bonds).

The U.S. government bond market considers U.S. Treasury, agency, state and local (municipal) segments, according to the type of issuer.

U.S. government securities

i) Treasury securities

- T-Bills
- T-Notes
- T-Bonds
- TIPS
- STRIPS

Treasury securities—also known as 'Treasuries'—are issued by the U.S. Treasury Department[7] and are considered to be zero credit risk securities, since they are backed by the credit of the U.S. Government. Main Treasuries include T-Bills, T-Notes, T-Bonds, Treasury Inflation-Protected Securities (TIPS) and Separate Trading of Registered Interest and Principal Securities (STRIPS). How about each one of them?

T-Bills are short-term government securities with maturities of 4, 13, 26, and 52 weeks. They are zero-coupon bonds sold at a discount from their face value, whereas T-Notes are issued with maturities of 2, 3, 5, 7 and 10 years and carry an explicit coupon rate that is paid every six months. Likewise, T-Bonds are similar to T-Notes but with maturities more than 10 years (today only 30-years T-bonds are issued), and are non-callable. In turn, TIPS are securities with maturities of 5, 10 and 30 years whose principal is adjusted by changes in the consumer price index. They also carry an explicit coupon rate that is paid every six months. Finally, STRIPS were born in 1985, when the U.S. Treasury stopped issuing zero-coupon notes and bonds. In such year, it introduced the STRIPS program allowing certain dealers to create 'synthetic zeros' to meet investor demand. This way, a 10-year, six-month paying coupon T-Note can be broken down into 20 coupon strips and one principal strip that could be sold separately.

On the primary market, Treasuries are issued through an auction process where both competitive and non competitive bids are allowed. Right after their emission, on-the-run issues (the most recently auctioned securities) are ready to be traded in the OTC secondary market together with all the off-the-run issues on the market. Treasuries are quoted on the market as a percent of their par value, where a percent is quoted in fractions being each fractional unit equal to 1/32. This way, a quote of 96-12 means 96 and 12/32, which equals 96.375% of the par value. For a bond with $1,000 of nominal value, a quote of 96-12 means it is sold on the market at a price of $963.75.

[6] As opposite to equity assets, nearly all of the daily trading on bond markets takes place in OTC markets, whereas just a few bonds, primarily corporate, are listed on exchanges.

[7] See <www.ustreas.gov>.

U.S. government securities

ii) Federal institutions

- *Ginnie Mae* securities

iii) GSEs

- *Fannie Mae* securities
- *Freddie Mac* securities

ii) Local governments

- *Munies*

Finally, in the U.S. not only the Treasury is responsible for issuing government debt securities, but also Federal institutions, State and local governments. To illustrate, Federal institutions like the Government National Mortgage Association (*Ginnie Mae*) or Government Sponsored Entities (GSEs) like the Federal National Mortgage Association (*Fannie Mae*) and the Federal Home Loan Bank Corporation (*Freddie Mac*) can issue government debt securities. The first type is backed by the full faith and credit of the U.S. government, so it is considered free from credit risk. Those coming from GSEs were considered to expose investors to very little risk until global economic meltdown caused Fannie Mae and Freddie Mac's severe crisis, and they had to be placed into conservatorship of a Federal institution. Finally, municipal bonds (*munies*) are issued by state and local governments. Most of them are tax-exempt.

In the case of the Eurozone, first to be noted is that the E.U. institutions have no fiscal budget on their own, hence there are no securities issued by the E.U. but by each individual country. Recently, the possible effects a Greek default would have on the euro currency, have increased positive opinions on issuing sort of 'E.U. Treasuries', but so far this is just speculation. Therefore, to illustrate, we shall analyze the government bond market for a European country, namely Spain.

Spanish government bonds:

- Letras del Tesoro
- Bonos del Estado
- Obligaciones del Estado
- Strips
- Repos

Spanish Tesoro Público issues securities—quite similar to those sold by the U.S. Treasury—that are negotiated at the Spanish *Mercado de Deuda Pública Anotada del Banco de España*. They include *Letras del Tesoro*, which are short-term zero-coupon bonds with maturities of 3, 6, 12 and 18 months, and face value of 1,000 Euros; *Bonos del Estado*, quite similar to Treasury notes, issued with maturities of 2, 3 and 5 years and pay an annual coupon; *Obligaciones del Estado* carry an explicit coupon rate—like Bonos—with the only difference of maturity (10, 15 and 30 years); *Strips*, similar to those in the US market in order to create 'synthetic zeros', such that from a 5-year Bono, 6 strips could be obtained; and *Repos* (repurchase agreements) which are investments in government securities purchased by the investor to a financial institution for a period of less than one year to maturity, such that the seller commits to re-buy it back later on. Agents commonly agree to carry out repos for very short periods of time, like one day ('overnight') or several days, usually fifteen at most.

Example 3

Table 2. Spanish government debt, last auctions available on June 10th, 2011

	IRR	Coupon	Maturity	Auction
Letra 3m	1.38%		19/08/2011	24/05/2011
Letra 6m	1.77%		18/11/2011	24/05/2011
Letra 12m	2.55%		18/05/2012	17/05/2011
Letra 18m	3.10%		19/10/2012	17/05/2011
Bono 3A	4.04%	3.40%	30/04/2014	02/06/2011
Bono 5A	4.23%	3.00%	30/04/2015	02/06/2011
Oblig.10A	5.40%	4.00%	30/04/2021	18/05/2011
Oblig. 15A	5.67%	4.80%	31/01/2024	20/04/2011
Oblig. 30A	6.00%	4.70%	30/07/2041	19/05/2011

Source: <www.tesoro.es>. (m: months, A: years).

Above we can find all on-the-run Spanish government securities available on June 2011. Considering that data we can plot them on a graph in order to have an idea of which yield curve[8] we could find on the Spanish market...

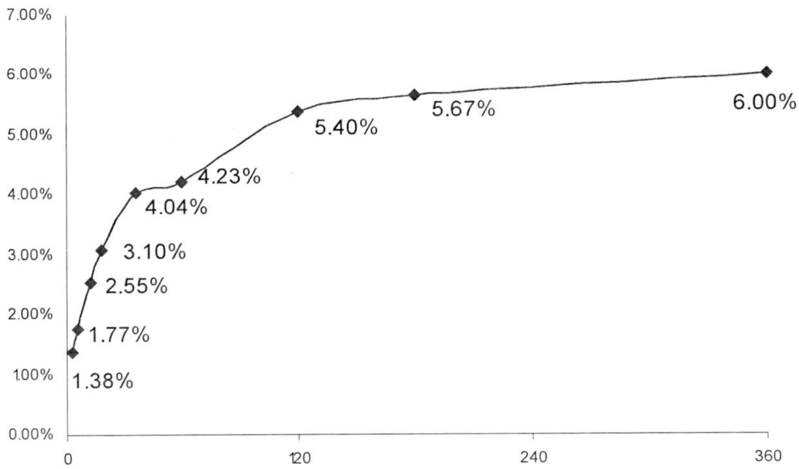

Source: <www.tesoro.es>.

Figure 6. A yield curve?

... but we must be aware that the Term Structure of interest rates is obtained using data for all maturities at the same time, and these on-the-run securities have been issued on auctions ranging from April to June 2011. Unfortunately, as we shall see later on, obtaining the yield curve is not that simple.

[8] The yield curve is an important concept we are going to see next in this chapter. We shall learn then that here in this example we are not using the correct data to plot the yield curve.

3.3. CREDIT MARKETS

Though government securities are the core of debt markets, they are not the only assets traded there. Many corporations sell private securities in order to finance their operations. Most of them are short-term issues like commercial paper, commercial bills or note issuance facilities considered to be money, as we saw in chapter 2 above, but private firms also issue corporate bonds and medium-term notes with maturities larger than a year that are traded on debt markets.

Corporate finance[9] studies the financial decisions a company must take in order to maximize its value while dealing with all financial risks. Choosing long-term investments and deciding whether to finance them with equity or debt are essential decisions to make. Companies finance their investments issuing equity shares that are to be traded on stock markets, but they can also chose to increase their debt by selling corporate bonds on the market. Corporate securities have the same properties as government bonds, but investors willing to buy them will require a higher interest rate of return on them because there is a probability that the company would not be able to fulfil its obligations.

Hence, an essential concept arises: credit risk. Bondholders can lose all or part of their investment if the issuer defaults. The probability for a U.S. government bond to default is considered to be zero, but any privately issued security should pay a higher return than its equivalent Treasury bond with the same maturity in order to compensate for the risk of default. And this compensation should be higher the greater the credit risk of both the issuer and that specific emission.

Commercial rating agencies like Fitch, Moody's and S&P provide a rating (a measure of the quality of the issuer given by letter designations) for any corporation or government institution, and for every single issues by those agents, too. A typical scale uses the following ratings: AAA, AA, A, BBB, BB, B, CCC, CC, C and D (the latter for debt already in arrears), being AAA the highest rating (meaning minimum risk) and D the lowest. Assets from AAA to BBB categories are said to be 'investment grade' bonds, whereas those with lower rating are known as 'non-investment grade', 'speculative grade' or junk bonds.

The 'four Cs' of credit quality:

- Character
- Capacity
- Covenants
- Collateral

In order to determine a company or an issue rating, credit rating agencies analyze the so-called "four Cs" of business credit quality: character, capacity, covenants and collateral.

Character is related to the company's management quality and depends on factors like size, location, number of years in business, business structure, quality of control systems, long-term strategies, financial policies, etc. Capacity, or the ability of the business to pay its bills, depends on cash flows and the structure of the company's debt. Covenants are the set of

[9] We shall have a closer insight of corporate finance in chapter 4 below, when we deal with equity markets.

constraints imposed on the borrower on the contract whereas collateral is the asset pledged by a borrower to secure a credit in case of default. Finally, depending on whether there is or not a collateral securing a corporate bond, we distinguish secured debt (debt plus collateral, in form of either financial assets or real property) and unsecured debt (that is, debenture bonds raised without any collateral that depend only on the borrower's credit worthiness).

There exists a third way to increase the credit quality of an issue, through credit enhancements where either the asset is guaranteed by a third party, or where a bank issues a letter of credit that ensures the quality of the borrower. Also we should mention two types of securities that are similar in a way to secured debt with collateral in form of real property, asset-backed securities (ABS) and mortgage-backed securities (MBS). As we have seen[10], the former are securities whose cash flows depend on a pool of credit card balances, auto loans, etc. The idea is that the borrower can get a better credit rating on a specific debt issue—and hence reducing its cost of financing—by securitizing[11] some assets on its balance in order to dedicate their cash flows to that particular security. MBS, on the other hand, are similar to ABS but they are backed by pools of mortgage loans, which provides both with collateral and the cash flow to pay the debt on the security. Finally, a specific type of ABS[12] is given by the so-called collateralized debt obligations, CDOs. In a CDO investors are divided into a number of asset classes, and how principal repayments are channelled to different classes is determined by specific rules agreed in advance[13].

3.4. Bond Valuation and Risks Associated with Investing in Bonds

Debt investments are easier to value than, for example, equities because they exhibit some fixed features that make then follow specific paths. More clearly, bond valuation is tied at maturity by the redemption value at the end of the investment, whereas the price during the life of the bond depends on interest rates. Relevant factors to determine quoted prices are four: the interest rate on the market for similar securities and maturities, the term to maturity of the principal, the size and frequency of the coupon payments and the face value of the bond. This way, the price P today of a bond of maturity n would be the present value[14] of all payoffs, including the redemption value at the end of the investment. Formally,

$$P = \sum_{t=1}^{n} \frac{C_t}{(1+r)^t} + \frac{N}{(1+r)^t}, \qquad (7)$$

where C_t is the coupon being paid at time t, r denotes the interest rate of the market and N the redemption value at the end of the investment. In this equation we are assuming that the

[10] Recall in section 3.1 above the taxonomy of fixed income assets.

[11] In simple words, securitization is the practice of pooling loans and/or mortgages in an investment vehicle, and sell them as bonds.

[12] Besides, collateralized mortgage obligations, CMOs, are a specific type of MBS.

[13] For more info, see Hull (2000).

[14] For those not familiar with financial calculation, the present value of any future cash flow is mathematically expressed by simply dividing the cash flow by $(1+r)^n$, where r is the appropriate discount rate that measures the 'cost of time' or 'opportunity cost' of money invested, and n is the number of periods considered.

discount rate, *r*, is the same for all maturities. This is an assumption that, as we will see in subsection 3.5, is not that realistic. So when we have different interest rates for different maturities, we usually do the opposite: if we observe the price of the bond at the market, using equation (7) we solve for the single discount rate, *r*, such that the equation holds. Such rate is known as the internal rate of return.

Equation (7) shows there is an inverse relationship between quoted price and return. As interest rates on the market increase, the price of a bond will decrease, and vice versa. This relationship is not linear but convex, meaning bond prices go up faster than they go down, as we see in figure 7.

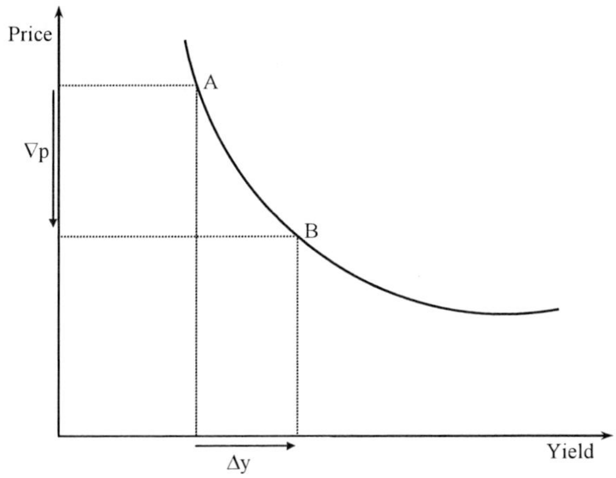

Figure 7. Price to yield curve of a bond.

Debt investments are 'fixed income' securities because their relevant features, such as the maturity, the coupon rate or the frequency of payments, are determined in advance and cannot be modified later on. But this does not mean bonds are risk free, not at all. Since interest rates on the market move 'randomly', one should be aware that bond prices are neither constant nor even that smooth as a naive investor would believe. As the saying goes, *fixed income is not that fixed*. Further than that, bonds are exposed to several sources of risk and should be evaluated in terms of the return they offer per unit of risk. In what follows we are going to mention six different types of risks, and the effects of each one of them on the behaviour of bond prices.

Risks associated with investing in bonds:

- Interest rate risk
- Reinvestment risk
- Liquidity risk
- Credit risk
- Yield curve risk

First and straightforward risk is the interest rate risk. As equation (7) for the price of a bond indicates, any variability on market interest rates will affect the bonds market value in an inverse proportion: if interest rates increase after a fixed-rate bond has been issued, then its quoted price will fall. This can be easily understood when considering that right after interest rates have risen, for the newly issued bonds to be sold at par they have to carry higher coupons. Older bonds, carrying a lower coupon rate, will become unattractive to investors unless their price drops to a point where it matches the return on new bonds. The opposite will happen when interest rates fall.

This inverse relationship between interest rates and bond prices is determined by three factors: the term to maturity, the coupon rate, and the existence or not of embedded options. Regarding the term to maturity, bonds with longer maturities will be more sensitive to interest rate changes. This is because—see equation (7)—cash flows that are further into the future are discounted strongly than the closer ones. The relationship between interest rates and the bond prices is also affected by the coupon rate, since bonds with lower coupon rates will have greater interest rate risk. This is so because the principal payment at the end of the investment will have greater weight when computing the price of the bond as coupons are smaller. Finally, embedded options make the future cash flows of a bond harder to predict. We are not going to get deeply into it, but just as an idea for readers, the call price on a callable bond acts as a 'ceiling' on its value, affecting the sensitivity of the bond price on changes on interest rates. Measuring this inverse sensitivity of bond prices to changes in interest rates is essential to investors, and duration[15] is the most widely used measure for such purpose. It is given by the expression

$$\text{Duration} = \frac{1}{2} \cdot \frac{\underline{V} - \overline{V}}{V_0 \cdot \Delta r}, \qquad (8)$$

where V_0 is the initial value of the bond, $\underline{V}$ is the price of the bond if the interest rate increases in Δr, and $\overline{V}$ is the price of the bond when interest rate decreases that same amount. Different duration measures sum up two different approaches to estimate the sensitivity of a bond price: modified duration, for example, measures the sensitivity of the bond price to changes on the interest rate—it would be calculated as the first derivative of the bond's price with respect to yield—whereas Macaulay duration represents the weighted average maturity of the bond's cash flows, providing a measure of the 'average life' of the bond. Since it is a positive measure, the price change of a bond, ΔP, due to an increase or decrease in interest rates is calculated as

$$\Delta P = -\text{Duration} \cdot \Delta r. \qquad (9)$$

Finally, duration is related to most of the determinants of a bond price. In particular, it can be shown duration moves inversely with both the coupon rate and the yield to maturity (that is, the higher the coupon rate or the yield to maturity of the bond, the lower its duration), whereas the longer the time to maturity, the higher the duration. On the contrary, the forth determinant of a bond price—which, as we have seen, is the face value of the bond—has no effect over its duration.

Duration is anyhow a limited measure. This is so because though it is a linear estimation of price sensitivity, the price to yield relationship of a bond is actually curved, as depicted in figure 8.

[15] We are using here the effective duration to measure the duration of a bond. Other duration measures commonly used are Macaulay duration and the modified duration (the latter calculated by dividing Macaulay duration by $1+r$).

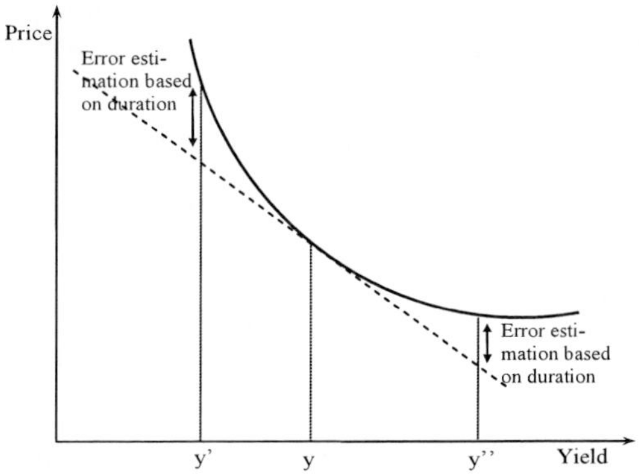

Figure 8. Error estimation based on duration.

The larger the yield variation, the larger the error in estimating price volatility using just the duration formula. This problem can be solved by estimating the degree of convexity (the second derivative of the price function with respect to yield), using it to help duration for a more accurate estimation of the change in a bond price.

$$\text{Convexity} = \frac{1}{2} \cdot \frac{\underline{V} + \overline{V} - 2V_0}{V_0 \cdot (\Delta y)^2}. \tag{10}$$

Risks associated with investing in bonds:

- Interest rate risk
- Reinvestment risk
- Liquidity risk
- Credit risk
- Yield curve risk

The second risk involved in bonds investment is the so-called reinvestment risk. When we say a bond yields an internal rate of return of, for example, 5%, we are assuming that all cash flows generated during the asset life are reinvested at that rate until the maturity date, which clearly cannot be ensured. Reinvestment risk is the probability, bored by the bond holder that the cash flows generated before the maturity date (coupons, and also the principal for amortizing bonds) will have to be reinvested at a lower rate than the promised yield on the bond. As well as interest rate risk, reinvestment risk is higher the longer the maturity of the bond. On the contrary, bonds with lower coupons will have greater interest rate risk, but lower reinvestment risk.

Risks associated with investing in bonds:

- Interest rate risk
- Reinvestment risk
- Liquidity risk
- Credit risk
- Yield curve risk

Investing in bonds also faces liquidity risk, meaning the difficulty for an investor to sell it quickly and without any loss in price. Liquidity risk can be estimated through the bid-ask spread on quoted prices for a specific bond. Callable or pre-payable bonds have also prepayment risk: investors may find their deal cashed before maturity, and must find another place to invest their money. From the bondholder's perspective, a called bond means not only a disruption in cash flow but also a sharply reduced rate of return.

Risks associated with investing in bonds:

- Interest rate risk
- Reinvestment risk
- Liquidity risk
- Credit risk
- Yield curve risk

Another relevant source of risk (perhaps the most important besides interest rate risk) is credit risk, which was already described in section 3.3. Credit risk is actually a combination of three sources: default risk, credit spread risk, and downgrade risk. Default risk is the probability of a debtor's failure: lenders face a higher risk the lower the credit quality of both the borrower and the security. Credit spread risk, on the other hand, holds because riskier investments require higher yields than the equivalent government bond. Credit risk gives a measure for that extra required return. For example, if a three-year T-Note yields a 3%, and an equivalent three-year private security yields a 4%, then the credit spread would be 1%. Credit spread risk is thus the risk that the credit spread will increase, causing the value of the issue to decrease. It has the same effects as a change in the market interest rate of the same proportion. Finally, downgrade risk refers to the possibility that either the issuer or the security would be downgraded by credit rating agencies. As we have mentioned before, credit risk depends on the quality of the seller, its capacity to pay, the presence and credit quality of collateral and the legal guarantees and requirements set by the covenants on the indenture.

Risks associated with investing in bonds:

- Interest rate risk
- Reinvestment risk
- Liquidity risk
- Credit risk
- Yield curve risk

Finally, readers might notice the yield curve risk. This source of risk comes from the volatility of interest rates as we have seen in the interest rate risk section. There we saw the price of a bond varies inversely to changes in interest rates on the market, but we must realize that there is not a single interest rate on the market, rather virtually 'infinite'. The interest rate market consists of a structure of interest rates, one for each maturity term. That structure is called the yield curve or the term structure of interest rates, as we are going to see next.

3.5. Term Structure of Interest Rates[16]

Recalling the formula to calculate the price of a bond[17], there is no such thing as a single interest rate r. Instead, a different discount rate applies to each cash flow payment. Hence, one could consider a bond is made up of a bunch of separate zero coupon bonds, one for every coupon and principal payments[18], and valuing such bond would be done by calculating the sum of all present values for every zero coupon bonds. This exposure to different yields is known as the yield curve risk of a bond or portfolio. Thus, no single measure of duration can

---

[16] For simplicity, we are going to use as synonymous two slightly different concepts in practice: the term structure of interest rates and the yield curve. Properly speaking, the term structure would be constructed using the yield to maturity on zero-coupon bonds, whereas the yield curve could be obtained for any type of fixed income securities, by simply calculating the yield to maturity of bonds of the same family with different maturities, and plotting them on a graph. Term structure and yield curve are only equivalent for zero-coupon bonds, but anyway the yield curve is usually used as an approximation for the term structure of interest rates.

[17] See equation (7).

[18] Remember that is what they do with STRIPS securities.

be used to estimate the price volatility due to changes in the yield curve. This leads to the concept of rate duration, where the sensitivity of the bond price to a specific rate in the term structure, all the rest constant.

The yield curve is the relationship between the observed interest rates on the market and their term to maturity, where yields are plotted on the vertical axis, and maturities horizontally. We could find a yield curve for securities with similar features (similar credit risk, liquidity, etc.), but usually yield curves for treasuries on each currency and market are calculated, and non-treasury required rates of return are derived from them. Interest rates paid at a particular point in time on treasuries are observed for each maturity, so the term structure is actually only known for maturities where bonds are available on the market, while the rest of the curve is calculated by interpolation[19]. We can illustrate this in the following figure.

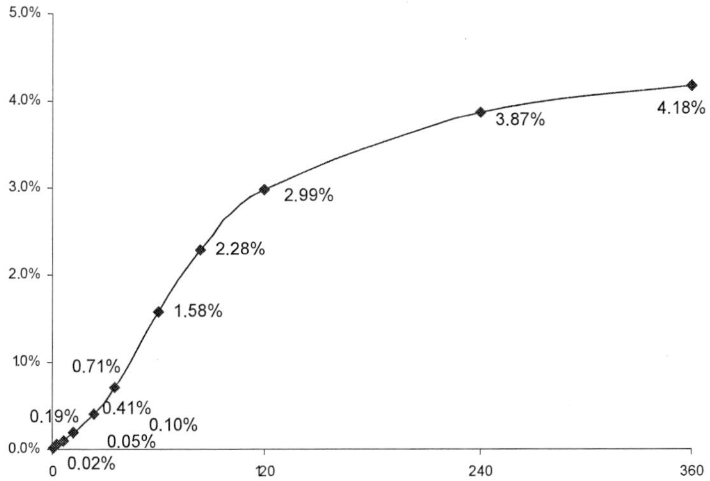

Source: www.ustreas.gov.

Figure 9. The U.S. yield curve on June 10th, 2011.

Instead of plotting all on-the-run government securities data at the time of their emission, as we wrongly did before when talking about the Spanish government market[20], we must gather all available data on both on-the-run and off-the run issues on a particular day, observe their yield to maturity for all of them, and plot that data against their time to maturity. Strictly, the term structure of interest rates is calculated using only the zero coupon bonds on the market, and interpolating for the rest of the maturities. In practice, since we have few observations—especially in certain markets and for medium and long-term investments—the curve is obtained through a sample of yields for issues with various maturities and difficult to standardize, calculating then a least squares regression to estimate the curve.

Finally, when studying the behaviour of the yield curve, market analysts focus attention on two relevant concepts. The first one is the shape of the yield curve: normal yield curves are upward sloping, with greater rates for long-term maturities. Liquidity preference theory,

[19] Interpolation is a mathematical method to calculate new data points in the middle of a given set of known data points. In our case, interpolation is useful to determine, for example, the 7-month interest rate when 6- and 8-month interest rates are known.

[20] See section 3.2 above.

where investors require higher returns on long-term investments because they find them riskier, would be an answer for such characteristic. Besides, a flat curve is the situation where yields on all maturities are essentially equal, and an inverted yield curve would be the one with a negative slope. In practice, the slope or steepness of the yield curve is described by rate spreads between different maturities.

The second issue is concerned with changes the yield curve can experiment with the passage of time. Under a parallel shift, yield on all maturities experiment a change in the same direction by approximately the same amount, and the slope of the curve remains unchanged. On the contrary, with a non-parallel shift, yields oscillate in a different proportion, and the slope varies. Non-parallel shifts fall into two categories: twists, where the slope of the curve becomes either flatter or steeper (flattening or steepening twists), and butterfly shifts that affect the curvature of the term structure.

Chapter 4

EQUITY MARKETS

Stock exchanges are the quintessential financial markets. Probably, before buying this book, many readers not versed in the topic would identify financial markets just with stock exchanges (it is really not such a coincidence since, matter of fact, Wall Street is an icon of our era).

We have mentioned that long-term assets are traded in capital markets, and among them, we differentiated fixed income securities traded on debt markets from equity investments traded on stock exchanges. In equity markets, shares representing owner-ship stakes of the issuer are traded. Now, throughout this section, we will give a description of those assets, the structure and main characteristics of stock exchanges and how to operate in them. Later, in part II of this book, we will also provide an insight on how to evaluate those investments.

4.1. CORPORATE FINANCE

First of all, readers must understand why companies choose to sell their shares on exchanges. As the activity of a company goes forward, managers analyse different investment alternatives as they arise, deciding where to invest, and getting the best sources of financing to execute previously chosen projects. Financial statements—that is, balance sheet and income statement—provide CEOs[1] with straightforward tools to analyze the situation of the company, its strengths and weaknesses, the investments ongoing and the financial needs both in the short and the long term. The area dealing with such investment and financing decisions is called corporate finance.

Table 3. Balance sheet of a company

Assets	Liabilities
Current assets	Liabilities
- cash	- current liabilities
- account receivable	- long-term liabilities
- inventory	Equity
Fixed assets	- capital stock
	- retained earnings

The balance sheet of a company is summarized in table 3. Assets are the means a company has to perform its activities. Liabilities, on the other hand, are the sources used to finance company's assets. This way, the capital structure of a company is the way it finances its assets through a combination of equity and debt. Franco Modigliani and Merton Miller stated that, under specific conditions, the value of a company does not depend on its capital structure. But we know from 'real life' that deciding whether new investments should be financed issuing new shares or engaging in more loans is a basic responsibility of a company's board of directors. The Modigliani-Miller prediction works under stringent assumptions like the absence of transaction costs, taxes or bankruptcy costs, and considers there is no information asymmetry among agents. All quite unrealistic, because when creditors lend money to corporations, is common that stockholders will benefit from risky strategies that simultaneously increase the probability of success and bankruptcy. Since the manager receives the full benefit of success but the creditor bears the risk of a bankruptcy, moral hazard appears so an agency problem[2] arises. Modigliani and Miller also considered the possibility for more realistic situations, finding out that, when company taxes and insolvency costs are accounted, there exists an optimal combination of equity and debt that minimizes cost of funding.

This most realistic point of view considers there exists an optimal capital structure that maximizes the company value: on one hand the cost of debt is generally lower than the cost of capital, but on the other both the cost of debt and the required return on shares by the company owners are not constant, but increasing with the possibility of default (which is correlated with the leverage of the company). This way, there will be an optimal capital structure—denoted by L^* in figure 10 below—for moderate levels of indebtedness such that the average cost of capital is minimized, maximizing the company value. Managers of the company should try both to minimize the cost of all sources of financing, as well as to identify which combination of equity and debt maximizes the value of the company.

[1] Chief Executive Officer, i.e. the managing director of a company.

[2] An agency problem (or a principal-agent problem) arises when one person (the principal) hires another (the agent) to take a decision that concerns the former, but a conflict of interest appears because the agent acts to pursue her own interests (and the principal cannot observe such actions).

Another example of the importance of capital structure is the working capital, a concept that provides a measure of a company's capacity to develop its activities normally in the short term. Whenever a company's current liabilities are bigger than its current assets, it faces a liquidity problem that jeopardizes its continuity. Therefore, capital structure decisions should consider too much short term debt could be risky. The same idea is behind the habit of many companies to finance most of its balance through capital and reserves because they are longer term, which provides more stability since a leveraged position increases risk. But, on the other hand, they should not forget self-financing has an implicit cost—the required rate of return on capital, K_c —, which is higher than the cost of debt K_d ($K_c > K_d$, which here we consider constant).

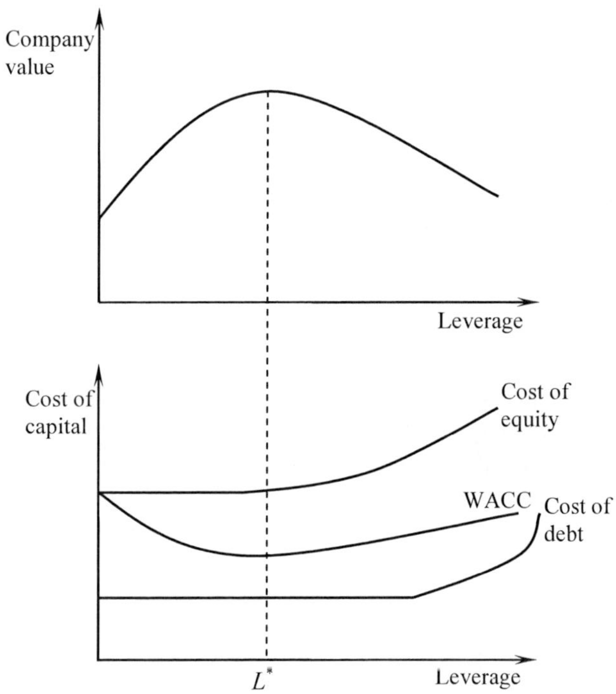

Figure 10. The optimal capital structure.

As a conclusion, as long as a company is able to generate a return well above that level and its leverage is balanced, seeking external funding looks reasonable in order to increase profit while decreasing the weighted average cost of capital (WACC). The simplest expression of WACC for a company financed with capital at a required rate of K_c and debt at a rate K_d is given by

$$\text{WACC} = (1-\alpha)\cdot K_c + \alpha \cdot K_d \cdot (1-\tau), \tag{11}$$

where parameter α, $0<\alpha<1$, measures the leverage of the company (the amount of debt to total assets) and τ represents the tax rate.

Therefore, there is rationale for a company either to raise debt or issue new capital to finance its operations, and so the choice between debt and capital will depend on their cost and the company preferences at any time. We have seen in section 3 that, if they choose debt, companies can look for it on debt markets, but when they prefer capital, where do they get it from? A nice option for them would be looking for it at stock markets, a set of institutions linking savers and investors that allow companies to find new stockholders. The efficiency achieved will be the greater the higher the flow of savings conveyed to productive investment and stock markets have proved essential for this purpose.

For companies, being listed on exchanges involves a number of advantages: namely, they have access to more diversified sources of financing, and usually at a lower cost, it improves the company's public image, offering a free source of advertising, and it creates an incentive for greater professionalization of management, opening the possibility to design incentives for employees through stock options[3]. Issuing stock could be an alternative when the company has not enough capital and prefers not to go to debt markets, either because it cannot count on such long term funding, or it finds debt price too expensive, or simply because of a corporate policy that considers an increase in the capitalization of the company should be promoted. But, on the other hand, companies should not forget stock markets could also be discouraging, because issuing new equity implies a loss of power to former stockholders, and greater transparency on equity markets impose requirements on companies such as external auditing, fiscal controls and information reports.

Equity markets make the process of issuing new stock easier for companies, since they improve their quality increasing liquidity and transparency, supporting investors' confidence. There, companies issue capital in pieces each one known as a share—a legal title that represents a stake on the capital of a company—which provides the holder with the right of voting at the annual general meeting of shareholders, the benefit to participate in dividends and the assets of the company in case of liquidation, and preferential subscription rights in case new shares are issued. Formerly, shares were represented by physical certificates, but nowadays they are usually recorded just electronically.

Types of shares:

- Ordinary shares
- Preferred shares
- Non-voting shares

Shares—together with subscription rights on stock right offerings—are the main assets traded on stock exchanges. Depending on rights they bear, we may distinguish ordinary, preferred and non-voting shares. Ordinary shares—also called common stock or equity—embody all economic and political rights mentioned above. Preferred shares are hybrid instruments that resemble properties of both equity and debt. They are senior to common stock in case of company liquidation, but subordinated to bonds[4]. Finally, non-voting stock refers equity that does not have political rights. Preferred stock typically has nonvoting qualities too. We can also differentiate nominative shares from bearer shares—being the latter unnamed—and shares issued at par, at a premium or on a discount, whether their issuing price is equal to their nominal value, superior or inferior.

[3] See Amat (2000), Blake (2000), and Pisón (2001), among others.

[4] Senior means 'they go first' in case of the company being liquidated, whereas subordinated means they get their money after bondholders.

4.2. STOCK EXCHANGES

By stock markets we refer to either a physical place or a network where trading of company stocks takes place. When transactions occur through entities that provide facilities for an organized trading, we talk about stock exchanges. Formerly they were physical venues, but in modern markets most of the operations are actually traded through electronic networks whereas trade on marketplaces is reserved for a few members only. Besides, there are many competitors—especially in the U.S. and the U.K.—that can negotiate the same way they do on stock exchanges: transaction services businesses that create their own Multilateral Trade Facilities, Electronic Trading Networks and so on. As an example, in London the London Stock Exchange (LSE) accounts today for only about the 60% of total volume negotiated there[5].

According to Bloomberg's world market cap index[6], the size of the World's stock market was about 53 trillion dollars by February 2011. Contrary to what happens with bond transactions, most of this volume is negotiated through exchange markets, basically at the International Federation of Stock Exchanges[7], which includes 69 exchanges in more than 40 countries. Anyway, stocks listed on a registered exchange may also be traded without going through the exchange. These transactions are called to be the 'Third Market'[8].

Example 4

Comparing the size of the World's stock market with the World's GDP, we find they are somewhat similar: \$62 trillion in 2010 for the World's GDP measured by IMF[9].

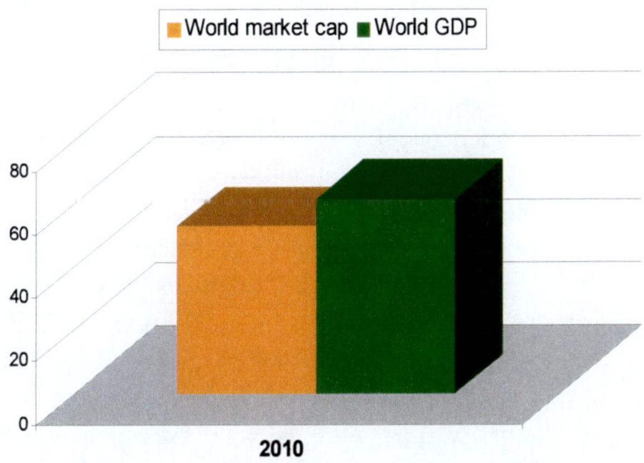

Figure 11. World market cap vs. World GDP.

[5] See Domowitz (1993). We gratefully acknowledge Domingo J. García-Coto from BME Research Department for providing this piece of information.
[6] See <http://www.bloomberg.com/apps/quote?ticker=WCAUWRLD:IND>.
[7] Source: <www.world-exchanges.org/>.
[8] Recall this definition in section 1.5.
[9] Source: <http://www.imf.org/external/data.htm>.

And we must be aware that, though all market economic activity would be recorded on GDP statistics, only traded companies compute on the stock market index!

Stock exchanges require securities to be listed there in order to trade them, so when there is an inability to meet listing requirements, usually brokers and dealers negotiate them directly among each others. Such off-exchange trading is called over-the-counter (OTC). In the U.S., the New York Stock Exchange (NYSE) is the most well known stock exchange, while the National Association of Securities Dealers Automated Quotation (NASDAQ) was born as the most famous OTC market, though today it is an official and regulated exchange as well[10].

On exchanges the main division we identify is the differentiation between primary and secondary markets. Primary markets are the place where securities are sold for the first time, facilitating capital formation. We talked before, on the corporate finance section, about companies that required new capital for financing their ongoing investments. When they want to issue new stock, they do it through a process called underwriting, where they hire a dealer or investment bank to help them selling their new shares to investors in an initial public offering (IPO).

On the other hand, secondary markets are those where the securities are traded once they have been issued. Whereas on primary markets investors buy company's shares directly from issuers, on the aftermarket they buy and sell the equity stocks one to each other. The relevant idea here is to understand that without a secondary market, primary markets would not succeed. Companies are keen on primary markets because they provide them with the financing required, but without the investors interest they would collect nothing. It is on the secondary market properties where savers find the attractiveness of investing: they provide readiness, liquidity to buy or sell quickly without additional cost, information on stock prices and trading volume—useful to have a clue on business valuation—and fast execution and settlement of orders.

Types of agents in stock markets:

- Capital seekers
- Suppliers of capital
- Intermediaries
- Regulatory agencies

In stock markets four types of agents intervene: capital seekers, suppliers of capital, intermediaries, and regulatory agencies. By capital seekers we mean those agents—mostly private corporations—looking for the financing they need. On the other hand, suppliers of capital are people or institutions willing to put their savings surplus in investment vehicles that provide them with the highest possible return at minimum risk, ensuring at the same time they can be sold quickly when required. Intermediaries are the agents that connect supply and demand for stocks, and include dealers—who can trade on their own—and brokers—agents that act only for others. Finally, regulatory agencies are responsible for the supervision of securities markets, by preserving transparency on the markets and ensuring investor interests.

Stock markets play seven essential functions for the good functioning of capitalist economies[11]. We can summarise them as follows.

[10] We thank Domingo J. García-Coto from BME Research Department for providing this piece of information.

[11] See Amat (2000) and Martín-Marín et al. (1991).

> **Seven functions of stock markets:**
>
> - Convey savings to investments
> - Allow participation on corporate governance
> - Facilitate liquidity
> - Means to determine securities prices
> - Provide info to investors
> - Guarantee purchases and sales
> - Barometer of the economy

First, they convey savings to investments, putting in contact agents with surplus savings and companies seeking to finance their long term investment projects. Second, they allow participation on corporate governance. Agents interested in taking part in the governance of an enterprise can do it buying stocks, since they have political rights, but in practice most shareholders are only interested on earnings and do not participate on management. Third, stock markets facilitate liquidity. In fact, if shares are easily converted back into money, more savers will be willing to finance corporations. Secondary markets are essential due to this property, because they allow to match issuers' time horizon (very long term) and savers (usually shorter). Besides, as we shall see in part II of the book, investors require to mobilize their portfolios in search of the highest return for a minimum risk, so the higher the liquidity of financial markets, the better.

Another essential role of stock markets is that they provide a means to determine a security price—hence giving an estimate of a company value—through supply and demand for stocks. Fifth, stock markets also provide investors with information, and dissemination of information is an essential requirement for financial markets to be efficient[12]. Stock markets provide data on prices, volumes, company financial statements and/or market indices that investors can use to take decisions more effectively.[13] Sixth, they provide a legal framework where all purchases and sales are guaranteed. Besides, enforcing that the same information is available to all agents at the same time helps promoting confidence. This way, one of the responsibilities for regulatory agencies such as the Securities and Exchange Commission in the U.S. is to avoid insider trading. Seventh, stock markets act as a barometer of the economy. In fact, stock markets, with their ups and downs, are considered to be a good indicator of future economic trends. Crashes—as we have checked recently—are usually a warning of an economic crisis to come.

Perhaps the best way to experience what stock markets really are would be visiting the NYSE facilities at Wall Street for a day. Anyway, we will try our best: along this section and the next one we would like to provide our readers with a basic description of how securities are traded, timetables and procedures, the different ways available to issue new shares and how to send and settle market orders, so you can come up with a basic picture of what a day on a stock exchange would be.

All stock exchanges are composed of a series of participants, trading mechanisms and an operational structure that can be summarized in five categories. Participants are the members of the stock exchange, that is, any authorized agent or any person or institution through authorized agents. Brokers, dealers and credit institutions are the only entities authorized to buy or sell securities on the exchange, enter market orders in the electronic trading system, participate in the clearing and settlement processes and act as depositary institutions. Related

[12] In part II of the book we shall analyze what financial markets 'efficiency' means.

[13] It should be noted that the two latter functions (promoting confidence and the stock markets as barometers of the economy) closely depend on whether stock markets are efficient or not.

with this, operating agencies are responsible to maintain a fluent functioning of markets, providing the facilities needed such as buildings, computers, communications, legal and administrative services, research, and so on.

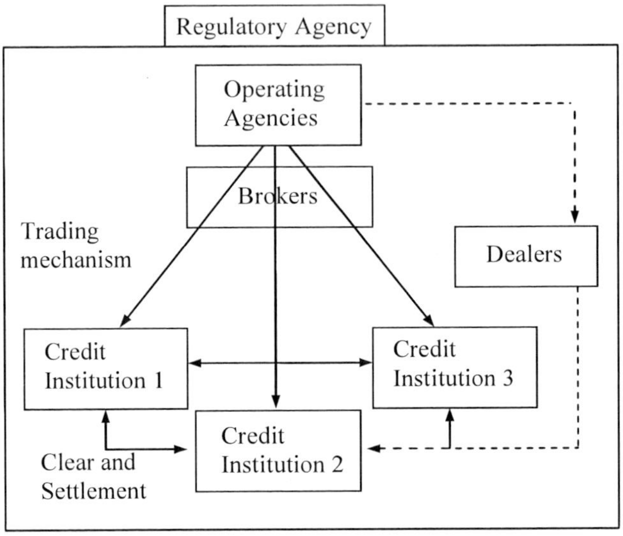

Figure 12. Structure of a stock exchange.

Regarding the trading systems, most of them are electronic devices, though open outcry on the trading floor of some stock exchanges also takes place. Clearing and settlement systems, on the other hand, are necessary because trading is much faster than the time required to endthe underlying transaction. Clearing involves ensuring that trades are settled in accordance with market rules, netting of trades to single positions, reporting and monitoring, whereas settlement is the process of delivering the securities against payment. Usually all these processes require a few days to be set, so for example it is said to be D+3 when it takes 3 days for a transaction to be successfully completed since the day the security was purchased or sold.

Finally, regulatory agencies provide markets with mechanisms for monitoring, legal services and control. They preserve transparency and ensure investor interests. In the U.S. the regulatory agency is the above mentioned Securities and Exchange Commission (SEC).

4.3. Securities Trading and Corporate Operations

On stock markets we observe most transactions conducted through normal daily trading, but from time to time some relevant operations could appear that are most of them related to corporate movements affecting a specific stock. We will start this section by examining normal securities trading, leaving corporate operations to the end of the section.

Securities Trading

On securities trading two ways of trading are available: open outcry and electronic trading. Open outcry—which has been the usual procedure until the appearance of the latter—is conducted through an open auction among trading professionals on the exchange, buying and selling specific securities during regular trading hours. All this results into the typical image we have of an exchange: investment professionals shouting and signalling in the middle of the trading floor. In the last two decades this system has been replaced almost entirely by electronic trading.

In 1971 NASDAQ became the world's first electronic stock market; in 1977 the Toronto stock exchange developed the computer assisted trading system (CATS), one of the first technologies that allowed for a full automation of the price-setting process as an assistance to open outcry; gradually, most exchanges around the world have been converting to electronic trading: *Paris Bourse* and LSE in 1986, *Bolsa de Madrid* in 1989, Chicago CME in 1992, etc. Only NYSE opted for what it was its identity mark, and developed an hybrid market where brokers can either have their orders executed immediately through electronic trading or at the trading floor via the more traditional open outcry method. As late as year 2000 the NYSE still opened what it was its fifth trading room, the *Bond Room* at 30 Broad Street, but it was closed years after. In 2007, additional trading floor expansions at 11 Broad Street—the NYSE main building—added decades before were closed back, turning what it seems the definitive victory of electronic trading in the most symbolic of all stock exchanges.

Regarding electronic trading, most exchanges are computerized markets where stocks, bonds, currencies or derivatives are traded electronically in virtual market places. NASDAQ, ARCA (New York), GLOBEX (Chicago), CATS (Toronto), CAC (Paris), SIBE (Madrid), TAURUS (LSE), and others are all examples of electronic 'market places' around the world. Though open outcry is still relevant in some trading venues (like the hybrid market at NYSE, or the CME where it still accounts for near 30% of total volume), in most markets around the world electronic trading accounts for almost[14] or all[15] the negotiated volume. Electronic

[14] In Madrid more than 98 percent.

trading boosted trading and dissemination of information on real time, ensuring complete transparency on the markets.

During a normal trading session we differentiate three periods of time[16]: an opening auction period, a trading period and a closing auction period. During opening auction, limit orders are sent to the central system, no negotiations are allowed, and after a period—usually half an hour—a 'match price'—the price at which the maximum volume of orders is executable—is released, so continuous trading can begin. The trading period refers to the time when securities are traded as usual. Orders are sent to the system, and whenever a buyer agrees to pay the lowest ask quote on the screen, or either another willing to sell it agrees to receive the highest bid quote, a new price for the stock is released. A normal open session develops continuously for a few hours. Finally, closing auction consists of a single-price Dutch auction (the auctioneer begins with a high ask quote which is lowered until a bid is accepted) that matches buy and sell orders at the price that maximizes the amount of tradable stock. This auction is usually shorter and lasts just a few minutes (just one in the NYSE, for example).

During trading hours several types of orders can be sent to the system. Most of them are regular orders ready to be matched at any time, and liquidated within a few days. They determine the official price of a security at any time, but not all of them are market orders to be executed at the best price available, so the central computer will maintain an electronic file, called the Book, through which orders are displayed and matched. Regular orders are received in real time, and are recorded on the Book respecting the priorities of price and reception time.

Types of orders in stock markets:

- Market orders
- Limit orders
- Inside limit orders
- Reserve orders
- Adding liquidity orders
- Fill or kill orders

The most relevant types of orders are six: market orders, limit orders, inside limit orders, reserve orders, adding liquidity orders and 'fill or kill' orders. Market orders are those where either a purchase or a sale is to be executed at the best price available at that moment. Limit orders stand for those in which an offer to buy or sell the security is sent at a specified price. Inside limit orders are orders matched at the best obtainable price for all the volume available, but any residual volume will not be routed to the next price level. Reserve orders are those with hidden volume, where agents make public only part of the volume they are actually willing to negotiate, and the limit order replenishes its size as executions are received until all the desired quantity is fully traded. Adding liquidity only orders are limit orders sent to the system by a market maker in order to add liquidity. Lastly, fill or kill orders are to be executed in full as soon as the order is received, or the entire order will be cancelled.

Example 5

Imagine bid and ask offers for Telefónica (TEF) shares are quoting as follows...

---

[15] In Toronto, the TSE's trading floor closed in 1997.

[16] Source: <www.nyse.com/equities/>.

size	BID	ASK	size
100	16.400	16.410	25
50	16.395	16.415	10
50	16.390	16.420	100
8	16.385	16.425	65
120	16.380	16.430	200

...meaning the highest offer to buy 100 shares is at a price of 16.4 euros, whereas the lowest price any agent at the market is willing to sell shares (25 shares in this case) is at 16.41 euros. Imagine now we wish to sell 160 shares of TEF. At which price will we be able to sell them if we use the different types of orders described above?

A 'market order' would be executed at the best price available at that moment. That means we would sell 100 shares to the agents willing to buy at 16.400 euros, another 50 at 16.395 and the last 10 shares at 16.390. With a 'limit order' we would specify at which price we are willing to sell. For example, if we wish to sell at 16.405 we would top the ask offers—as no other ask price would be lower than ours—but no shares would be sold until a bid comes to the market agreeing to buy at that price. Instead, if we send an 'inside limit order', the first 100 shares would be sold at 16.400 euros, whereas the other 60 (the residual volume) would be offered at that level instead of matching the next bid offers.

Now imagine the top bid (the offer to buy 100 shares at 16.400) is actually a 'reserve order'. In this case, though we see on the screen that agent (or agents) is willing to buy 100 shares, some volume is hidden. Think for example this agent actually wishes to buy 200 shares, but only claims to be ready to buy 100. This way, if we place a market order of 160 shares as we did in our first example, we would end up with all our shares sold at 16.400. The highest bid available to the market after our transaction would be 40 shares to be bought at 16.400.

Finally, what would happen if we send a 'fill or kill order'? Since this type of order is to be executed in full or cancelled otherwise, the result of our transaction would depend on whether the highest bid is a 'limit order' or a 'reserve order'. This way, if we send a 'fill or kill' order to sell 160 shares at 16.400 euros, and the highest bid is a limit order (that is, there are really only 100 shares to be bought), our transaction will be cancelled. But if that bid is actually a 'reserve order', since there are actually 200 shares available at that level, our sale would be executed in full.

Finally, as opposed to regular orders, some transactions are not sent to the electronic system and thus they do notcompute for quoting the official security prices. Those transactions are allowed to be executed, under specific regulation, for mergers and acquisitions, large transactions, the execution of option contracts, etc. Some of them could require special authorization.

Corporate Operations

Occasionally, we might observe some relevant transactions on the market that are most of them related to corporate operations affecting a stock price. The most important to mention are initial public offerings (IPOs), seasoned equity offerings (SEOs), mergers and acquisitions (M&A), convertible bonds, dividends and splits. IPOs are market transactions where the owner of a significant portion of a company's capital is willing to sell it on the market at a pre specified price. They imply the issuer sells common stock to the market players for the first time, such that a new company goes public. It may involve issuing new shares or not, in which case neither an increase nor a decrease of shares takes place, but a change in ownership.

SEOs are new equity issues by a company already listed on the exchange. It may involve shares sold by existing shareholders or actually issuing new shares—a transaction also known as 'capital increase' in which case the offering would be dilutive, meaning the reduction in ownership percentage and earnings per share former stockholders would experiment. On the contrary, capital decreases occur when the capital on the company's balance sheet is reduced. Mergers and acquisitions (M&A), on the other hand, are growth strategies, involving either the combination of two or more existing companies or the purchase of one by another. Acquisitions, also called takeovers, may be friendly—where both companies negotiate—or hostile, where the one being purchased is unwilling to be bought.

Finally, some other relevant company decisions that could affect a stock price are the issuing of convertible bonds, the payment of dividends and the decision to undertake stock splits. Convertible bonds are hybrid securities, that is, bonds that pay at first a usually lower coupon rate than the market, but in return they offer the possibility to be changed into equity at some future date at a pre-specified conversion price. The company gets a low-cost source of financing and a possibility to convert debt into equity, but in exchange convertible bonds have dilution properties. Dividends are a variable compensation paid to shareholders as a result of distributing the company's profit. From the investor's side, it represents the main source of return and the most important reason for them to purchase stock. From the company point of view, it involves deciding what to do with its earnings, whether to pay dividends, retain earnings or repurchase its own stock on the market. And last, stock splits divide up each existing share into multiple ones, whereas the stock price drops so there is no change in the company value. Companies use splits to keep their quoting prices on the exchange at a trading level that they find more suitable, but they have no other valuable effects.

Chapter 5

OTHER FINANCIAL MARKETS

Money markets, bonds, and equity securities are the core of financial markets. They account for the majority of the wealth invested and for much of the transactions being executed. But yet, there are plenty more fish in the ocean! Currencies, derivatives and other alternative investments represent a growing proportion of financial markets. Foreign exchange markets have multiplied exponentially their trading volume with the increasing internationalization of domestic economies and the liberalization of exchange rates. The necessity for hedging risks gave rise to derivative instruments, which grew dramatically in importance as a result of speculation and the development of financial engineering products. And both the growing interest in having more investment choices, and the diversifying properties that the inclusion of alternative investments have on the overall risk of a portfolio developed vehicles such as hedge funds, private equity, venture capital, real estate and commodities.

In next section we shall have an insight on these three components. Since a more detailed study—especially for the derivatives section—would require higher technical skills and mathematical knowledge than the average reader would have, we will only provide a brief description of these markets and instruments on them.

5.1. FOREIGN EXCHANGE MARKETS

All transactions within a domestic economy are carried out in that country's currency. But different countries usually have different currencies, so any transaction between two or more agents working across countries will require the transfer of purchasing power denominated in one currency into another. The foreign exchange market (also named Forex market or FX market) is an OTC electronically linked network, where banks, brokers, and dealers trade amongst themselves determining the rate at which two currencies would be exchanged on the market at any time.

We said money markets, bonds and equity securities are the core of financial markets. They are indeed, but it is also true that the FX market is the largest, most efficient and most liquid financial market in the world. This is so because due to increasing internationalization of market economies and the globalization of capital markets, a growing share of market transactions are executed between countries and require a FX transaction to settle them. The

Bank for International Settlements accounted as of April 2007 an average daily turnover of \$3.21 trillion in FX markets[1]. This volume is the sum of four types of operations: commercial trading, where companies buy and sell goods and services between countries with different currencies; investment operations in financial products worldwide, since today agents invest in money market, fixed income, and equity securities no matter which country they come from; hedging operations; and speculative transactions. All of them require a price at which any two different currencies are exchanged, and these prices are quoted on the interbank foreign exchange market.

The FX market is open worldwide 24 hours a day. Currency pairs are quoted on the main markets around the globe, starting in Asia (Tokyo and Hong Kong, mainly), then forward to the Middle East and Europe (London, Frankfurt and Zurich) and ending in America (mainly New York, Chicago and Toronto). Since all pairs are quoted at any time and by many different agents at the most important venues worldwide, information is available to all market participants, and arbitrage[2] activities ensure quotes of one currency against the others tend to be equal in all markets. The FX market is therefore considered to be highly efficient, probably the most efficient of all markets.

Table 4. ISO currency codes

CODE	CURRENCY	COUNTRY
AUD	Australian dollar	Australia
BRL	Brazilian real	Brazil
CAD	Canadian dollar	Canada
CHF	Swiss franc	Switzerland
CNY	Chinese yuan	China
EUR	Euro	Eurozone
GBP	Pound sterling	United Kingdom
INR	Indian rupee	India
JPY	Japanese yen	Japan
KRW	South Korean won	South Korea
MAD	Moroccan dirham	Morocco
MXN	Mexican peso	Mexico
RUB	Russian rouble	Russia
SAR	Saudi riyal	Saudi Arabia
SEK	Swedish prona/kronor	Sweden
USD	United States dollar	United Sates
XAG	Silver	
XAU	Gold	
XPT	Platinum	

[1] Bank for International Settlements. Source: <http://www.bis.org/publ/rpfxf07t.htm>. (Data available for the 2007 survey (April'07).)

[2] By arbitrage we mean taking advantage of mispricing across different markets by selling assets that are overvalued, and simultaneously using the revenues of that sale to buy similar assets in other market that are undervalued. This way we make a riskless profit out of this trade without investing any money of our own.

ISO 4217 is the international standard for three-letter currency codes, where the most relevant are shown in table 4 above. Using those codes, currency pairs are quoted as one currency per unit of another, where the first one is said to be the 'quoted currency' and the one on the denominator is named the 'base currency'. The most common currencies are typically quoted this way:

- U.S. dollar per euro (USD/EUR)
- U.S. dollar per British pound (USD/GBP)
- Euro per British pound (EUR/GBP)
- Japanese yen per U.S. dollar (JPY/USD)
- Swiss franc per U.S. dollar (CHF/USD)

In order to avoid mistakes, market participants have agreed a series of conventions to express currency pairs and their bid and ask quotes. We see them next.

Conventions on FX market:

- Two ways of writing a currency pair
- The prevailed point of view
- Direct quotes, indirect quotes and cross rates

How to Write a Currency Pair

Since there are both a bid and an ask quotes, and prices on forex transactions are stated in terms of one currency per one unit of another, we must state clearly which currency is being purchased and which one is being sold. Since there are two ways to write a currency pair, if we write the currency codes before the quotes, the convention says the first currency is the one being purchased.

Example 6

If we see

EUR/USD 1.3305 bid 1.3320 ask

it means the highest bid on the market to buy one euro is $1.3305, whereas the lowest price offered to sell it is $1.3320 per euro. This is the way financial institutions commonly state currency quotes, and the way we see them on the screens.

We might also write the codes after the quoted price. But in this case, convention compels to write the base currency at the end. This way, a quotation of 1.3305 USD/EUR means we can trade $1.3305 for one euro. Amateur investors must be aware of these inverse notations. If we see a quotation for the euro against the U.S. dollar changing from EUR/USD 1.33 to EUR/USD 1.34, it means the euro is going up from $1.33 per euro to $1.34. But if quotes change from 1.54 USD/GDP to 1.55 USD/GDP, now quotes are in terms of 'U.S. dollars per one British pound', such that it has been the GDP the currency the one that went up from $1.54 to $1.55.

Figure 13. Currency exchange rates on a screen.

Conventions on FX market:

- Two ways of writing a currency pair
- The prevailed point of view
- Direct quotes, indirect quotes and cross rates

The Prevailed Point of View

Convention says bid and ask prices are stated always from the point of view of the bank that is quoting, not from the costumer's.

Example 6 (Continued)

If we see on the screen

EUR/USD 1.3305 bid 1.3320 ask

the bank is willing to buy one euro in exchange of $1.3305, and offers to sell one euro in exchange of $1.3320. The ask price will be always higher than the bid, such that a margin profit for the bank appears.

Conventions on FX market:

- Two ways of writing a currency pair
- The prevailed point of view
- Direct quotes, indirect quotes and cross rates

Direct Quotes, Indirect Quotes and Cross Rates

Market convention has also determined that currency pairs are said to be on direct quotation only when they are expressed in terms of foreign currency per $1. Therefore, USD/JPY 94.05 is a direct quotation where 94.05 yens are equivalent to $1, whereas EUR/USD 1.3305 is an indirect quotation where $1.3305 are equivalent to one euro.

Both direct and indirect quotes involve the American currency. But what happens if we are interested in trading British pounds in exchange of euros? A cross rate is the exchange rate between two non-U.S. currencies. Using each non-U.S. currency quotes against the U.S. dollar, we must use the appropriate bid and ask quotes to compute the cross rate.

Example 7

If we are given

EUR/USD 1.3305 bid 1.3320 ask

and

USD/JPY 94.05 bid 94.10 ask

the bid and ask quotes for the EUR/JPY would be the following: for the bid, in order to buy euros from yens the trader would buy U.S. dollars at a 94.05 USD/JPY rate and then use them to buy euros at a 1.3305 rate. Hence, the EUR/JPY bid rate would be 125.1335 JPY/EUR (94.05 multiplied by 1.3305). Whereas with respect to ask, it affords, doing the same algebra, an ask price of EUR/JPY 125.3412. Triangular currency arbitrage will take place whenever a cross rate out of its fair value generates an opportunity for a market participant to get a risk-free profit on it. Hence, FX markets are highly efficient, since we can get information about a currency from several cross rates, with arbitrage forces driving them to meet their equilibrium price at every moment.

Things on the FX market can get much more complex. When currencies are traded for immediate delivery, they are said to be exchanged on the spot market, but they can also be traded on the forward market for future delivery, usually in 30-, 90-, 180- and 360-day periods. Finally, currency swap markets are simultaneous transactions where we buy (or sell) a currency on the spot market and sell (or buy) it through a forward contract. In this case, arbitrage between spot and forward markets applies through the forces described on the IRP[3]; since the only difference between exchanging currencies in the spot and forward markets is the time of their transactions, arbitrage must take time—represented by the interest rate—into account. We are not going much deeper in it, just mention that IRP theorem states that the forward exchange rate F may be expressed in terms of the spot rate as

$$F = S \cdot \frac{1 + r_1}{1 + r_2}, \tag{12}$$

Where r_1 is the interest rate on currency 1, r_2 the interest rate on currency 2, F the forward (½) rate and S the spot rate (in ½ terms as well). If the interest rate differential is not similar to the forward differential among exchange rates, then an arbitrage opportunity would exist

[3] For further reading on IRP (the interest rate parity) see Stein (1962) and Aliber (1973).

and investors would move funds from one country to another to get advantage of that risk-free profit.

Example 8

We may calculate how much a currency would be expected to appreciate against another if we are given interest rate on those two countries. That arbitrage is linked with variations on exchange rates due to international differences on interest rates is a fact that can be easily shown. Consider an American investor who plans in year t to invest \$$X$ during one year, and faces two possibilities: (a) to invest in U.S. one-year bonds, or (b) to buy euros, invest in French one-year bonds and then to convert the euros into U.S. dollars at the end of the holding period. If the interest rate in U.S. amounts to r, the former strategy affords the investor with \$$X\cdot(1+r)$. On the contrary, strategy (b) obliges to consider the euro-U.S. dollar current exchange rate, e_t. First, the investor obtains X/e_t euros, and whenever the interest rate in France is r^*, the investor will obtain $(X/e_t)\cdot(1+r^*)$ euros. Then, once converted these euros into U.S. dollars at the current exchange rate at the end of the year, e_{t+1}, it yields \$$e_{t+1}\cdot(X/e_t)\cdot(1+r^*)$. It is clear that both strategies afford the same return when

$$1 + r = \frac{e_{t+1}}{e_t} \cdot (1 + r^*) \,, \tag{13}$$

a relation that can be approximated as

$$\frac{e_{t+1} - e_t}{e_t} \approx r - r^* \,, \tag{14}$$

which is known as (uncovered) interest rate parity[4]. In words, national interest rate must equal foreign interest rate plus expected rate of depreciation of national currency. The negative relationship between exchange rate and national interest rate can be graphically illustrated as in figure 14.

In sum, the adjustment to expectations about exchange rate is responsible of the differences among international interest rates even though a free capital flow assumption is made. If $r=r^*$, then it follows that $e_{t+1}= e_t$, i.e. the current exchange rate between the U.S. dollar and the euro equals the expected exchange rate in the future. If r^* increases (decreases) and $r<r^*$ ($r>r^*$), then a currency depreciation (an appreciation) takes place.

Exchange Rate Risk

When investing abroad, we must consider several factors that are not relevant when investing in the domestic economy. Transaction costs, taxes and political risks, for example, would be three of them, but the most important source of risk for international investments is the exchange rate risk. That is, the probability that an adverse movement in the exchange rate would reduce the return from an investment.

---

[4] Uncovered interest rate parity because e_{t+1} is unknown when investment is undertaken in period t.

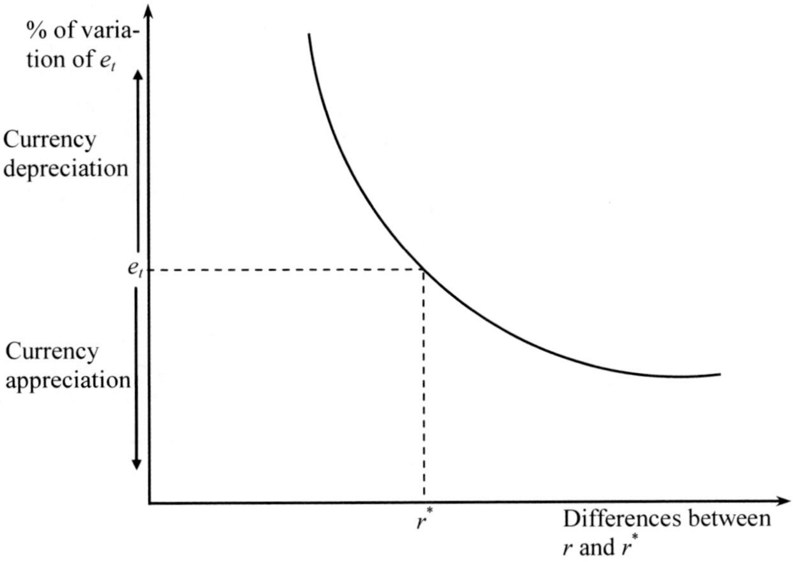

Figure 14. Interest rate parity.

Before 1973, exchange rates were driven by the Bretton Woods Agreement, a set of rules, institutions and procedures to regulate the international monetary system after 1944. The convertibility of the U.S. dollar into gold was set as $35 per ounce, and all the other countries committed to adopt a monetary policy that maintained the exchange rate of their currency pegged against the U.S. dollar within a narrow fluctuation band (plus and minus one percent) around the official exchange parity. During that period of fixed exchange rates, the main economic factor affecting currencies were balance of payments. Whenever an economy had a surplus on its balance of payments (because exports exceeded imports, for example), its currency would tend to appreciate, and the contrary happened when it showed a deficit.

But in August 1971 the U.S. authorities unilaterally terminated the convertibility of the dollar to gold, and the Bretton Woods Agreement broke two years later, in 1973. Since then, free floating for most currencies was set. Under free floating, exchange rates are determined by three types of factors: economic factors, political factors, and market sentiment. Economic factors refer issues such as the monetary policy (on interest rates, for example, and those interest rates as compared to other countries), budget and balance of trade deficits, economic growth, productivity, inflation rate, and the purchasing power parity of that country—a measure for the relative purchasing power of different currencies. On the other hand, political factors reflect whether there is a free market economy or interventionism, corruption or crony capitalism, and whether there is a high level of uncertainty in the political situation of such country or not. Lastly, market sentiment affects primarily to short term fluctuations on exchange rates, based on long term trends, technical trading, market expectations or flights to quality. In sum, extraordinary events that make investors look for a safe haven (a role that the U.S. dollar and gold have traditionally performed).

5.2. Derivatives Markets

"Derivatives are financial weapons of mass destruction, carrying dangers that, while now latent, are potentially lethal"
Berkshire Hathaway Annual Report for 2002 - Warren Buffett

Let us start mentioning an evidence: financial markets are risky. Investors face interest rate risk when investing on fixed income, market volatility when investing on equities, default risk when lending money to a private agent, exchange rate risk when investing abroad, and liquidity, legal and many other types of risks in any case. But not only financial markets are risky. For centuries, the main source of uncertainty for mankind was poor harvests and contingencies on trade. Therefore, people have always sought to avoid these risks, and... derivatives contracts were created for such purpose! In fact, we can find the origins of derivatives in early trade in Europe, which ended with the first forward contracts during the *Tulipmania*, or in Japan, 17th century, where the first standardized futures contracts were signed in the Osaka rice market.

The most significant event in the derivatives history was the creation of the Chicago Board of Trade (CBOT) in 1848. Chicago was a major centre for storage and sale of grain, but businesses had to bear high volatilities: prices tended to rise right after the harvest, since there were not enough storage facilities available at the same time, falling thereby after. To avoid this problem, contracts that set a price in advance for future delivery in Chicago were signed. Years after, CBOT offered standardized futures and option contracts on commodities like wheat, corn and soya, but counterparty credit risk was still a major concern. Finally, in

1925 the clearinghouse—an institution acting as an intermediary that guarantees all trades—was formed, at a time when financial derivatives were already available.

Derivatives are financial instruments whose payoffs depend on another underlying financial instrument or asset. Basic contracts allow to buy or sell the underlying asset in some future date, though more complex derivatives are also available. They are traded and quoted separately from the underlying asset, and generally settled in a future date. Contrary to equities and bonds, derivatives do not provide financing. Instead, their main virtue is that they allow to separate property and risk, that is, they allow risks on the underlying asset to be transferred from one party to another. For such reason, derivatives are used both for insurance (hedging risks on the price of the underlying asset) and speculative purposes (trying to profit from the future value of such asset). Hence, though derivatives were created to hedge risks, they are also used today for the contrary reason.

Types of derivatives:

- Futures and forwards
- Options and warrants
- Swaps

We can find basically three types of derivatives: forwards and futures, options and warrants, and swaps. Forwards and futures are contracts that determine today the price of an exchange that will take place at some future date. Basic differences between them are that forwards are tailor-made private contracts between two counterparties, so they face default risk, while futures are highly standardized agreements traded in organized exchanges among anonymous buyers and sellers that operate through the clearinghouse, which guarantees all transactions from default. In turn, options are derivatives that give its owner the right, but not the obligation, to make a transaction at some future date at a pre-specified price. For such right, the option buyer pays a price, called premium, to the option writer—the seller of the derivative—who has the obligation to perform in any case. Differences between options and warrants are generally akin to those between futures and forwards, though complex types of options—called 'exotic options'—are also traded at OTC markets. Finally, swaps are agreements to exchange cash flows over a period of time, based on the value of the underlying asset, generally either currencies or interest rates. We shall see them more in detail later on.

Some basic features are shared by all financial derivatives. For example, they provide agents with market completeness and price discovery, that is, plenty of information about all payoffs that can be obtained by trading the securities available at the moment and estimates on future prices. They allow as well market participants to engage in leveraged positions, earning large returns (or losses!) with small movements in the underlying asset's price. Since speculators try to maximize profits on their investments in the shortest period of time and providing the minimum possible funds of their own, one of the basic characteristics of derivatives contracts, their leverage, has been as well the reason behind the wide use of derivatives—initially designed to lessen risks—for speculative purposes. Anyway, both hedging and speculative transactions add to the completeness of markets.

Derivatives can be traded either on organized markets or on OTC markets. The basic distinction between them is that an organized market must have a clearinghouse—a financial institution that writes the contracts and intermediate between buyers and sellers—ensuring all transactions. The clearinghouse writes standardized contracts for specific assets and maturities, and reduces risks by netting offsetting transactions between multiple counterparties and requiring traders to make margin deposits and settle their accounts on a daily basis. Margins ensure traders will perform their obligations, and daily monitoring of such positions guarantees margins are updated according to the price movements on the underlying security. Organized markets permit an anonymous interaction between buyers and sellers, greater liquidity and lower credit risk with the drawback of rigidity (only contracts for specific derivatives features and maturity dates are available).

On the contrary, OTC markets have not a clearinghouse, so contracts are directly negotiated between the counterparties without any intermediary. Hence, the handicap is that for such contracts there exists credit risk. The advantage, they can be designed to fit all the agent's needs. Futures contracts and simplest equity options are exchange traded, while forwards, swaps and exotic options are basically traded in the OTC markets. Some of the major organized markets that trade with derivatives are Chicago Mercantile Exchange (CME), Chicago Board of Trade (CBOT), New York Mercantile Exchange (NYMEX), Hong Kong Futures Exchange, Eurex (Frankfurt), LIFFE (London) and MEFF (Madrid). In what follows, we briefly examine each type.

Table 5. Amounts outstanding in OTC derivatives

OTC notional amounts outstanding (in trillions of U.S. dollars)			
INSTRUMENT	**June 2007**	**June 2008**	**June 2009**
Total contracts	**516.4**	**683.8**	**604.6**
Interest rate contracts	**347.3**	**458.3**	**437.2**
- forward rate agreements (FRAs)	22.8	39.4	46.8
- interest rate swaps	272.2	356.8	341.9
- options	52.3	62.1	48.5
Foreign exchange contracts	**48.6**	**63.0**	**48.8**
Equity-linked contracts	**8.6**	**10.2**	**6.6**
Commodity contracts	**7.6**	**13.2**	**3.7**

Source: Bank of International Settlements 5.

Derivatives markets are more attractive to invest than securities markets, since they are more liquid, have lower capital requirements—engaging in leveraged positions—and offer lower transaction costs, resulting in greater trading efficiency. Data on derivatives traded around the world are an evidence of such huge success: in June 2009, the Bank of International Settlement[6] reported a notional amount outstanding of \$605 trillion in OTC derivatives plus more than \$70 trillion of notional amount outstanding in exchange traded derivatives, for a total turnover of \$1,660 trillion during year 2009.

Just compare these exorbitant figures with the world gross domestic product, estimated to be \$62 trillion in 2009, according to IMF[7]. This figure shows the immense volume traded on derivatives market, and gives us a good explanation of the damaging effect that failure of subprime mortgage derivatives recently had on international economies.

Derivatives are highly complex financial instruments, so a detailed study of all their technical aspects would require a much more advanced approach than required for this book. We can see on tables above there are several types of derivatives, such as forwards and futures, FRAs, CDS, equity options, currency swaps, commodity contracts... though in terms

[5] Source: Bank of International Settlements, <http://www.bis.org/statistics/otcder/dt1920a.pdf>.
[6] See <www.bis.org>.
[7] Source: IMF at <http://www.imf.org/external/data.htm>.

of volume the most used are those related to interest rates (swaps, futures and options). We will merely point out the basic features of these instruments and how to operate with them, inviting readers interested in further study of derivatives through any of the books recommended in the list of references at the end of the book.

Table 6. Derivatives in organized exchanges

Exchange traded derivatives (in trillions of U.S. dollars)					
INSTRUMENT	**Notional amounts outstanding**			**Total turnover**	
	Dec. 2007	**Dec. 2008**	**Dec. 2009**	**2008**	**2009**
Total contracts	**79.0**	**57.7**	**73.0**	**2,208.5**	**1,659.8**
Futures	**28.0**	**19.5**	**21.7**	1,543.7	1,126.1
- interest rates	26.7	18.7	20.6	1,392.6	1,016.3
- currency	0.2	0.1	0.2	24.4	24.2
- equity index	1.1	0.7	0.9	126.7	85.6
Options	**51.0**	**38.2**	**51.3**	**664.8**	**533.7**
- interest rates	44.3	34.0	46.4	526.6	434.6
- currency	0.1	0.1	0.1	2.8	2.0
- equity index	6.6	4.1	4.8	135.4	97.1

Source: Bank of International Settlements 8.

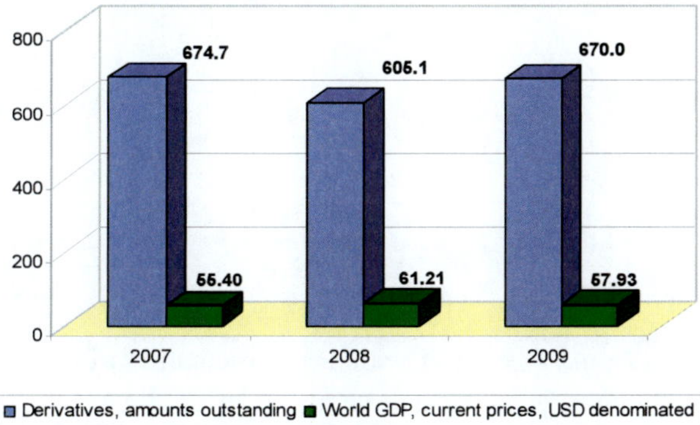

Note: Data on derivatives are at December 2007, December 2008 and June 2009.

Figure 15. Derivatives, amounts outstanding (in trillions of U.S. dollars).

Types of derivatives:

- Futures and forwards
- Swaps
- Options and warrants

Futures and Forwards

Futures and forwards are agreements between two parties in order to exchange a specific asset (known as the 'underlying asset') at some future date (the 'maturity date') for a price agreed in advance. Futures are standardized, traded on organized markets, and can be writable either on interest rates (the majority of them), currencies, stocks, stock indices and commodities. Forwards, on the contrary, are negotiated over-the-counter, and the most common are forward rate agreements (FRAs) and currency forwards. Futures and forward positions can be closed at maturity with the delivery of the underlying good—it is estimated, nonetheless, that less

[8] Source: BIS, <http://www.bis.org/publ/qtrpdf/r_qa1003.pdf#page=126>.

than one percent of all futures are settled through delivery—or at any time making a reverse trade that offsets the initial position.

Forwards and futures are valued in a similar way. Their payoff at maturity T could be easily represented with the formulas

$$\text{Payoff} = S_T - K, \tag{15}$$

for a long position (the value for the agent that buys the contract), and

$$\text{Payoff} = K - S_T, \tag{16}$$

for a short position (the value for the agent that sells the contract), where S_T denotes the price of the underlying asset at the spot market[9] and K the delivery price, agreed in advance.

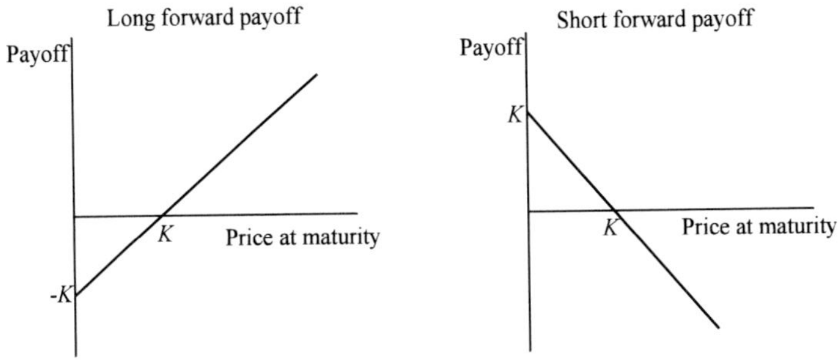

Figure 16. Futures and forwards' payoff at maturity.

Using either equations (15) and (16) or their representation in figure 16, it is easy to see that when the price at maturity of the underlying asset is above the pre-specified delivery price, a long position on a futures or a forward makes a profit, because the derivatives allow to buy the underlying asset at a price K, which is lower than its price at that time in the spot market. The contrary happens to a short position or to a long position when the spot price falls below the delivery price.

We shall better see it through an example.

Example 9

Mike has a portfolio of 1,000 shares of Microsoft (MSFT). Knowing he will need to sell the shares within three months in order to make some payments, he wishes to fix today the sale price in order to avoid future wailing. Visiting Andrea, his financial advisor, she offers him the possibility to buy or sell MSFT shares at $24 per share in that future date. Which position shall Mike take? Is he agreeing to buy/sell a futures or a forward?

---

[9] Since futures and forwards introduce the possibility to trade an asset in some 'future' date, we differentiate between futures markets and 'spot' markets, being the latter those where the asset originally trades (shares at stock exchanges, bonds at debt markets, etc.).

Since he wishes to sell shares, he must take a short position. Since the contract is among private parties, not anonymously through an organized exchange, this derivative is an OTC contract. Therefore, Mike should take a short position in a forward to sell 1,000 shares.

Which profit or loss will Mike and the bank get if at maturity date MSFT shares are quoting at the spot market at \$20, \$22, \$24, \$26, or \$28? We shall better see it graphically in figure 17.

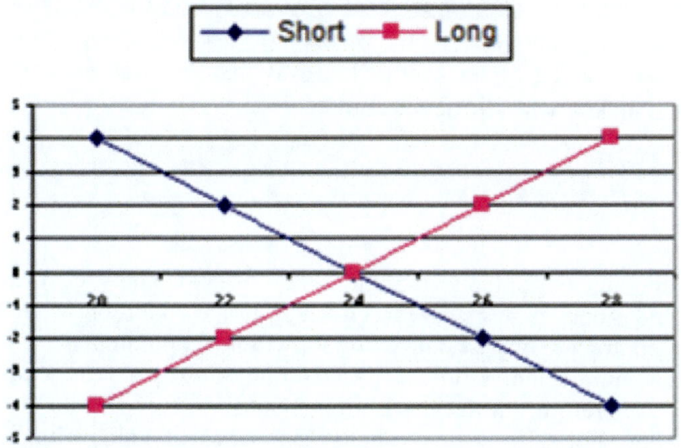

Figure 17. Payoffs on a forward on MSFT: Short and long positions.

For example, if MSFT shares quote at \$28, Mike loses \$4 per share (remember he agreed to sell for \$24 what eventually at maturity date in the spot market he could have sold for \$28) and the bank makes a \$4 profit on each share.

As we have seen in the example, the buyer and seller of a forward contract do not pay any price for the derivative at the agreement date, neither they shall pay for a futures contract. However, since futures are traded in organized exchanges, some sort of initial guarantee—a margin deposit—will be required. Therefore, what matters for both the buyer and the seller of a futures or a forward contract is to determine a delivery price that satisfies both parties. This, as in any other financial market, will depend on each agent's expectations about the future price of the underlying asset, as well as their bargaining power. But additionally, between spot and futures markets an arbitrage condition must also hold:

$$F_T = S_t + \text{Cost of carry}, \tag{17}$$

where F_T is the derivatives price, i.e. the delivery price agreed at time t to buy or sell the underlying asset at some future date T, S_t is the spot price of the underlying asset at the time of the agreement, t, and the cost of carry represents the cost of holding the asset from time t to T. Equation (17) provides a theoretical value at which bid and ask prices for a futures or a forward should agree.

Cost of carry can include the opportunity cost of money (measured by the riskless interest rate for that period[10]) and costs of transport, storage, custody and insurance, if we are dealing

[10] Recall the debt markets section and the interest rates for different maturities provided by the term structure.

with physical goods. If we make it simple, the theoretical value would depend only on interest rates, assuming all the other costs are negligible[11]. In such case, the arbitrage condition becomes

$$F_T = S_t \cdot (1+r_{t,T}), \qquad (18)$$

where $r_{t,T}$ is the risk-free interest rate at which we can lend or borrow from period t to T. Whenever this condition does not hold, an arbitrage opportunity (i.e. the possibility to make a riskless profit) arises. Any rational investor would like to take the opportunity to make such easy money. This way, market forces operate in a way that the arbitrage condition eventually holds. We will see it clearer with the next example.

Example 10

The price of an ounce of gold at the spot market is $1,500. Risk-free rate at which we can either borrow or lend money is 4% per year. Given arbitrage condition, what is the theoretical value of a forward contract to buy an ounce of gold within six months?

We will make it simple and assume a risk-free rate of 4% per year is equivalent to a 2% within six months. Therefore, the forward price should be F_T = $1,500·(1+0.02) = $1,530. The buyer and seller should agree to exchange an ounce of gold, within six months, for $1,530.

What happens if we observe forwards are quoting at some other price? How could we make a riskless profit out of it? Let's examine the two possible situations.

1. The forward price is 'too expensive'. Imagine F = $1,600, for example. What an arbitrageur should always do—and so any person with common sense!—is to buy low and sell high. Therefore, buying gold in the spot market and selling a forward contract should provide a riskless profit. We calculate it:
   - we borrow $1,500 for six months at 4% annual (2% for the six months), and with the money we got we buy an ounce of gold
   - we take a short position on a forward contract in order to sell gold within six months at $1,600 per ounce
   - within six months we pay back the loan: $1,500 plus interests, equals $1,530...
   - ...and settle the derivatives, selling the ounce of gold we bought six months ago in exchange of $1,600.

   We made a riskless profit of $1,600–$1,530 = $70. Since it would be such an easy money, any rational observer would do the same. Therefore, the increased supply of futures contracts would lower their price until futures and spot markets equilibrate.

2. The forward price is 'too cheap'. For example, imagine F = $1,400. Here we should buy a forward contract and sell gold in the spot market to make easy money. We calculate it:

[11] Not such a stringent condition when the underlying is a financial (not physical) asset.

- we borrow ('short-sell'[12]) an ounce of gold and sell it at the spot market for $1,500.
- we deposit those $1,500 during six months in a bank account at 4% annual (2% for the six months)
- at the same time, we take a long position on a forward contract in order to buy gold within six months at $1,400 per ounce
- within six months we receive the money we invested with interests: $1,500 plus interests equals $1,530...
- ...and settle the derivatives, buying an ounce of gold for $1,400.

We made a riskless profit of $1,530–$1,400 = $130. Again, any rational observer would do the same, so the increased demand of futures contracts would rise their price until futures and spot markets equilibrate.

In any case we must take into account that, in practice, the arbitrage condition provides a theoretical valuation that accounts for a fluctuation band rather than a unique value[13]. What is important here is to understand the implication of this arbitrage condition: since the futures market depends both on agents' expectations as well as the arbitrage relationship with the spot market, futures and spot prices are interrelated, moving together closely.

Finally, a particular case of special interest is given by forward contracts on interest rates, known as FRAs[14]. With FRAs, buyer agrees to pay a fixed interest rate, whereas the seller pays a floating interest rate, the underlying interest rate. At maturity both payments are netted so only the differential is paid. They are useful both for borrowers and lenders on loans or deposits to protect themselves from future changes in the reference interest rate on the loan or deposit. For example, borrowers paying a floating rate on their loan would be willing to buy a FRA if they expect interest rates to rise, and so would do lenders at a fixed rate. On the contrary, borrowers at a fixed rate and lenders at floating would choose to sell a FRA whenever they expect interest rates to fall. Forward exchange agreements, FXAs, work similarly, with the parties agreeing a specific exchange rate in advance in order to protect themselves from risk related to exchange rate fluctuations.

Types of derivatives:

- Futures and forwards
- Swaps
- Options and warrants

Swaps

Swaps markets have grown exponentially because they are a straightforward and low-cost way to manage interest rate and currency exposures. In fact, interest rate swaps account for about a half of all notional amounts of outstanding derivatives in the world today. Once he have seen forward contracts in the previous section, swaps are easy to understand. Swaps are OTC derivatives set as a sequence of forward contracts, with the purpose of protect ourselves from longer term risks. Though one can find swaps on stock and on many other different assets,

[12] Short selling in financial markets means to borrow an asset from a third party (usually a broker) to sell it at today's price, buying it back later to return it to the lender. It represents the inverse strategy of what an investor usually does: we try to buy low a stock today, hold it on during some time, and sell it when it is high to make a profit. A short selling strategy bets on the contrary: we sell now high, and wait for some time until the stock has, hopefully, loss some of its value to buy it back and return it to the lender.

[13] Reasons are, for example, that lending and borrowing rates are usually not the same, neither the prices at which we can buy or sell gold. Besides, short selling is not cost-free, but here we have obviated its costs.

[14] Forward rate agreements.

most common derivatives are plain-vanilla[15] interest rate swaps, and plain-vanilla currency swaps. Plain vanilla interest rate swap are similar to FRAs, with a party paying a fixed interest rate and receiving a floating rate based on the Libor, with the interest payments regularly exchanged on a net basis. Meanwhile, on currency swaps parties agree to exchange cash flows denominated in two different currencies. Plain vanilla swaps are those in which the floating rate cash flows are in dollars, and the fixed in any other currency. Since cash flows are denominated in different currencies, interest payments are not netted, and principal values are actually exchanged at the beginning and the end of the contract.

Types of derivatives:

- Futures and forwards
- Swaps
- <u>Options and warrants</u>

Options and Warrants

Options and warrants are derivative instruments that give the buyer the right, but notably not the obligation, to decide whether to buy or sell the underlying asset at some pre-specified date or period of time and at an agreed-upon price. Since they give the owner a right to exercise the derivative, she must pay a price on it. That makes options and warrants different from standard futures, forwards and swaps, and harder to price, as we shall see next.

Options and warrants can be written on interest rates, futures, stock, market indexes, commodities, currencies, and many other assets. As it happens with futures and forwards, options and warrants are similar derivatives, with the basic distinction that the former are standardized contracts traded at organized exchanges, and the latter are issued by private institutions. Warrants are tailor-made and generally traded over-the-counter[16]. Anyway, this distinction is not always clear when we can also find options that are traded over-the-counter (like exotic options we shall see later on). In what follows we will deal exclusively with options, describing several of their features and a basic introduction on option pricing, understanding that this description is essentially entirely applicable to warrants.

Standard options (plain vanilla) are of two basic types: call options and put options. Calls give the owner the right to buy the underlying asset at the pre-specified strike price, whereas puts give the owner the right to sell it. Since we have two participants—the owner, having the right to exercise the option, and the seller, obliged to perform—and two basic types of options, we can distinguish four basic positions: long call, long put, short call and short put.

Table 7. Options: Four basic positions

	CALL	PUT
Long	Right to buy	Right to sell
Short	Obligation to sell (if required by the buyer)	Obligation to buy (if required by the buyer)

Finally, we can also distinguish European and American options. European options are those where the owner has the right to exercise them only at maturity, whereas American

[15] Simplest standard derivatives (swaps, options, etc.) are called plain vanilla in the financial jargon.

[16] More detailed, warrants are issued either by financial institutions in order to organize a market on derivatives and sell them to their customers, or by private companies selling warrants on their own stock. This latter case is generically related to the emission of convertible bonds by the company (recall convertible bonds on the fixed income securities section).

options may be exercised at any time. Therefore, four basic positions (long and short call and put options) times two possibilities to exercise them (before or at maturity), that makes eight basic types of options. Those eight cases will be the focus of our analysis.

In order to analyze the different option positions and how to price them, it is useful—and simpler—to start characterizing European option positions in terms of the payoff to the holder at maturity. For example, for a long call, the payoff at maturity, C, also called intrinsic value, is given by the formula

$$C = \max\{S_T - X, 0\}, \tag{19}$$

where C is positive whenever the price on the underlying asset at maturity, S_T, is higher than the exercise or *strike* price fixed in advance, X, and zero otherwise. This is so because whenever the underlying asset price is higher than the price at which we agreed to buy it, we make a profit, but if the price is lower we will not exercise the option—otherwise we would lose money—so the payoff is zero.

The formula above is also representative of the intrinsic value of an option—whether European or American—at any time, just calculating the difference between the price on the underlying asset at any time t, S_t, and the strike price, if positive, zero otherwise[17]. Since the owner of the call has paid a premium[18] for having the right to exercise the derivative, the payoff and the profit of a long call could be depicted this way.

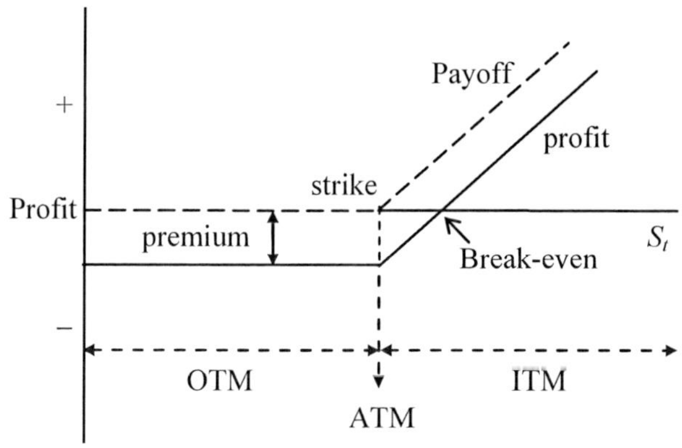

Figure 18. Payoff on a long call.

This would be the payoff for the investor buying the call option, with limited losses (equal to the price of the derivative) and potentially unlimited gains. Whenever S is above the strike price we say the option is 'in the money', meaning we would make some money if exercised (the payoff would be positive). This does not necessarily mean we have made a profit out of it, because the payoff could be smaller than the premium paid in advance. Anyway, any European option shall be exercised at maturity if it is ITM, whether or not we

[17] There is though a noticeable difference between using the payoff formula at any time before maturity or at maturity. As we shall explain later on, the value of an option is the sum of its intrinsic value and its time value. But at the expiration date, time value is zero. Therefore, equation (19) can be used to price options at maturity, but is helpless to price them at any time before maturity.

[18] We shall see later how to calculate it when we deal with option pricing.

make a profit, because we will always prefer to lose, say, half the premium rather than the whole premium. If the option is 'at the money' (ATM), S equals X and so the holder would be indifferent between exercise the option or not. Finally, if the option is 'out of the money' (OTM), meaning the underlying asset price is below the strike, the holder of the option shall not to exercise it. Let's see an example.

Example 11

On March 1st, we take a long position on a European call option on Pfizer, PFE. We pay a premium of \$1 for the right to purchase PFE shares at \$20 on June, 1st. When shall we exercise the option? What would be the payoff and the profit of our strategy if PFE is quoting at \$22 on the exercise date? What is the break-even point?

We shall exercise the option if PFE shares on June 1st are quoting above \$20. For example, if they quote at \$22, the payoff on the option will be \$2 (we are paying \$20 for something it is worth \$22 on the market), and our profit, including the premium paid on the option, will be \$1 (\$2 – \$1). The break-even point is the price on the stock that makes our profit zero, i.e. \$21, since at that point the payoff on the option would be \$1, equal to the premium we paid.

Opposite to a long position on a call, the investor selling the contract would face an inverse payoff at maturity, as illustrated in figure 20.

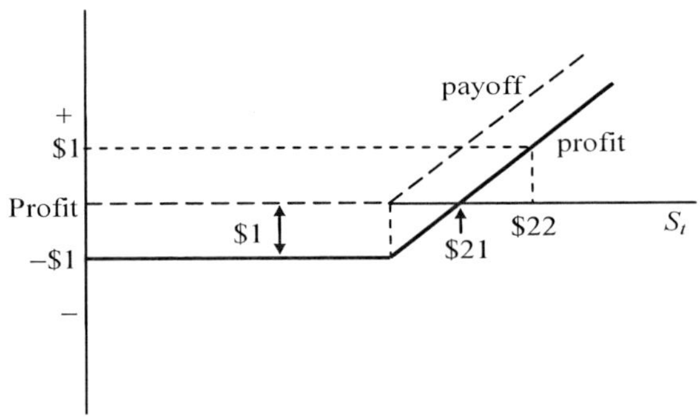

Figure 19. Intrinsic value and profit on a call.

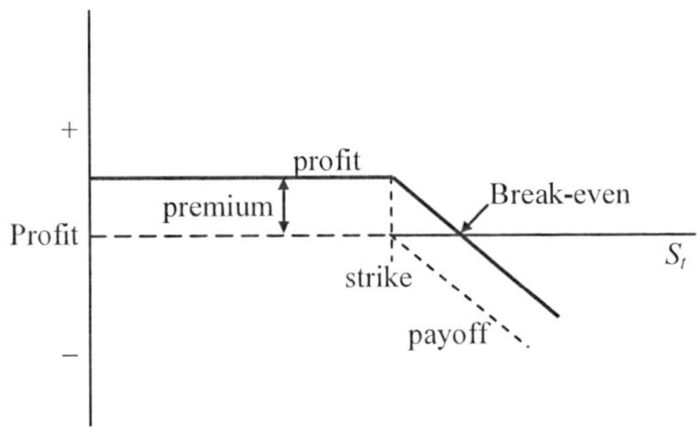

Figure 20. Payoff on a short call.

Investors might also like to bet that a stock's price is going to decrease in a short period of time. They should then buy a put option, which gives the right to sell—rather than to buy, as with call options—the underlying asset at an agreed-upon strike price. The payoff P at maturity of a long put is given by

$$P = \max\{X - S_T, 0\}, \qquad (20)$$

because if the underlying asset price is below the strike, the put option gives us the right to sell the asset at a higher price than it quotes on the market, whereas would the exercise price be lower, we would choose not to exercise the option. The opposite holds for a short position on a put. The graphical representation of both a long and a short put would be as follows:

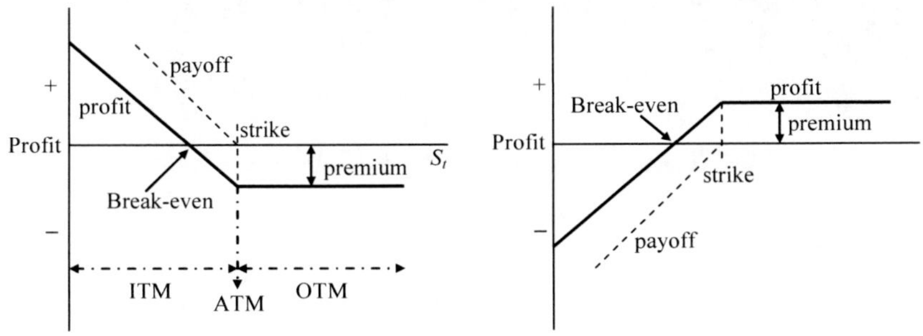

Figure 21. Payoff on a long and a short put.

Pricing options at maturity is feasible. It simply requires calculating its intrinsic value, as above. But at any time before maturity, things get much more complex. Generically speaking, the value of an option is the sum of two parts as stated in the following equality:

$$\text{Option price} = \text{Intrinsic price} + \text{Time value.} \qquad (21)$$

What does it mean options have time value? Think of a call option as in our example 10: on March 1st we wish to take a long position to purchase PFE shares at \$20 on June 1st. Imagine we do not know yet which premium should we pay to buy the option, but we know today PFE is quoting at \$19.5. The intrinsic value of the option is clearly null since, using Equation (19), $C = \max\{\$19 - \$20, \$0\} = \$0$.

But... can we say the option has no value at all? The option is to be exercised within three months—or, if we are to buy an American call, at any time within the next three months—so it is possible that PFE price rises during that period. It could happen that, though today it quotes at \$19.5, on June 1st it quotes at, say, \$21.5 and so the option would be in the money. We can see it clearer if we spin to the left the graph of the payoff on a long call we saw in figure 18, and represent time on the x-axis as in figure 22.

Starting at an initial value of $S_t = \$19$ the intrinsic value of the option on March 1st would be zero. But imagine that afterwards PFE share price follow the path depicted above. In such case, the final payoff on this call option would be positive. Therefore, whenever it exists a possibility of a call yielding a positive result at maturity, any rational investor would be willing to pay something for it, whether the intrinsic value of the option at the beginning is positive or not.

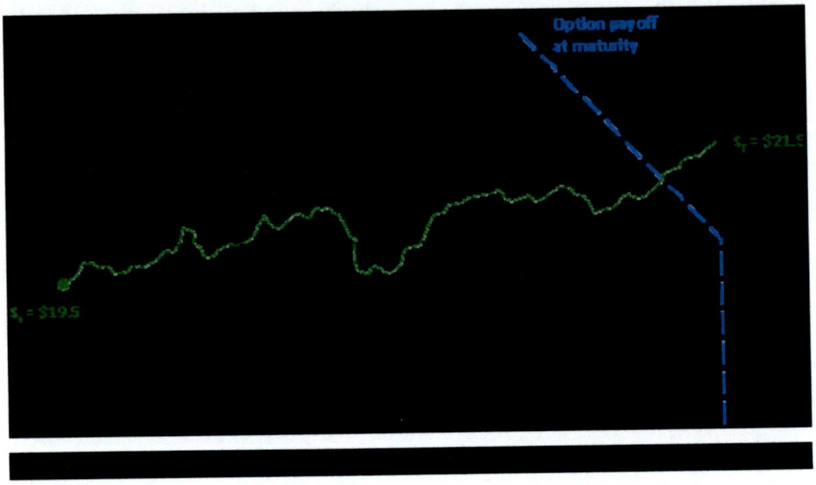

Figure 22. Time value of an option.

Any valuation model should account for the evolution through time of the underlying asset price. In particular, it should consider six essential variables that determine the value of an option: namely, the underlying asset price at present time, S_t, the strike price, X, the time to maturity, $T - t$, the volatility of the underlying asset price, σ, the time-cost of money, measured by the risk-free interest rate, r, and if the underlying asset pays some dividend or coupon, they shall be also be considered. Furthermore, any satisfactory model should also meet some simple features of option prices. For example, it is easy to see American options are worth at least the same as their equivalent European ones (since they allow for early exercise, we have more possibilities to 'win'). Therefore, an American option price should be equal or higher than the price on an European option with similar characteristics (underlying asset, time to maturity and strike)[19]. Similarly, it should be obvious a call option will be more expensive than another if either it has longer time to maturity or its exercise price is lower[20]. Obviously, the correspondent result for puts would be that we prefer higher strike prices. One additional condition that applies both for puts and calls is that the higher the volatility of the underlying asset price, the more valuable the option[21].

---

[19] Just mention here a classical result of option pricing: it could be proved an American call written on an underlying asset that pays no dividend will never be exercised before maturity. Therefore, in this particular case American and European call prices will be equal. This result does not hold for put options: an American put will be exercised if it is sufficiently deep in-the-money.

[20] Properly speaking, the 'maturity' condition holds for American calls. For European calls we may treat it as a usual condition, though some exceptions apply.

[21] This result is easy to see if we analyze figure 22. If between March 1st and June 1st PFE share price moves upwards there is odds the option ends up being ITM ($1.5 in our example above), whereas if it moves downwards, the worst thing it could happen to us is that the payoff would be zero (no matter what price below $20 we end up with, we will choose not to exercise the call). Compare that result with a similar call option but written on a more volatile underlying asset: if the asset price moves upwards, we have chances to make a higher payoff since the asset is more volatile, it could reach higher prices in the same period of time, whereas the worst thing it could happen to us is that, again, payoff is equal to zero if the asset price falls, no matter how

Finally, one essential arbitrage condition option prices must hold is the put – call parity condition

$$P = C - S + X \cdot e^{-r(T-t)}, \quad (22)$$

which can be rearranged as $P + S = C + X \cdot e^{-r(T-t)}$ for a better interpretation. That is, these two portfolios must always have the same value: a put option written on the underlying asset S plus a share of that stock on one hand, and a call option with similar characteristics as the put plus the net present value of the strike price on the other.

Those are basic properties any option pricing model must account for, but the mathematics behind those models goes far beyond the purposes of this book. For that reason, we shall only mention the most acclaimed option pricing model. In 1997 Robert Merton and Myron Scholes were awarded with the Nobel Prize in economics for the mathematical model Robert Merton published in 1973 based on a previous work by Fischer Black and Myron Scholes (Black and Scholes, 1973). That model is known as the Black-Scholes formula, and today is widely used in the financial industry to price European options. Assuming stock prices follow a stochastic process known as geometric brownian motion (GBM)[22], Black and Scholes provided a theoretical value for derivatives written on that stock as underlying asset. In particular, the formula proposed for pricing an European call would be

$$C(S,t) = S \cdot N(d_1) - X \cdot e^{-r(T-t)} \cdot N(d_2), \quad (23)$$

where $d_1 = \dfrac{\ln\left(\dfrac{S}{X}\right) + \left(r + \dfrac{\sigma^2}{2}\right) \cdot (T-t)}{\sigma\sqrt{T-t}}$ and $d_2 = d_1 - \sigma\sqrt{T-t}$, being C the price of the call option, S the price of the underlying security, $T - t$ the time to maturity, $N(\cdot)$ the cumulative distribution function of the standard normal distribution, X the strike price of the option, r the risk-free interest rate and σ the standard deviation (or volatility) of the underlying security price. Nice, isn't it?

Even nicer if we realize this is just the formula for the most basic European call. Pricing a European put[23] is quite similar,

$$P(S,t) = X \cdot e^{-r(T-t)} \cdot N(-d_2) - S \cdot N(-d_1), \quad (24)$$

but things can get much more complex for pricing American options, underlying assets paying dividends, exotic options, etc. And yet, the Black-Scholes formula is just an approximation for real world, since it is based on assumptions such as geometric brownian

much. Therefore, we will prefer options on volatile stocks, so they should be more valuable. An equivalent result should be obtained for put options.

[22] A stochastic process is a random process that describes the future evolution of a variable when uncertainty is involved to some extent. A brownian motion, on the other hand, is the assumed random movement of a particle suspended in a fluid (a liquid or a gas). Think of the feather in 'Forrest Gump', and you will have a good idea of what a brownian motion is. (The brownian motion was first formulated in 1905 by Albert Einstein.)

[23] Doing the maths, it can be easily proved equations (21) and (22) meet the put-call parity at any time, as we said it is required to any valuation model.

motion for prices and log-normal distribution for returns, no-arbitrage conditions, costless trading, constant volatilities over time, etc.

Complex Derivatives

Finally, we will just mention that apart from basic futures, forwards, options and swaps, we can find on the market many other more complex derivatives and combinations: swaptions (options on swaps), exotic options (asiatic, lookback options, etc.), option combinations (caps, floors, collars, butterflies, etc.), and many other structured products. An almost endless list!

We shall not go deeper into it[24]. But for readers' better understanding of a future chapter in this book, we do wish to give a little introduction on a complex derivative that played a relevant role in the recent financial crisis: credit default swaps (CDS). CDS are credit derivatives that give the holder the right to sell for its face value a bond issued by a company in the event this company defaults. In return, the holder makes periodic payments to the issuer of the derivative. Usually credit default swaps are settled by delivery of the bonds, but sometimes are settled in cash[25]. CDS—and CDOs, analyzed on the debt markets section—increased the risk appetite of investors and reduced the risk perception of financial institutions and supervisors. They were one of the factors that bred the worldwide crisis we recently witnessed, as we shall examine in part III below.

5.3. Alternative Investments

We are going to end part I of the book with some assets that are, some of them, non-financial. Since in part II we will examine how investors—willing to maximize the risk-return properties of their portfolios—tackle the analysis of all investments available, we would like to make our list totally comprehensive mentioning all the existing opportunities they can find on the markets. And not only because this would make our list more comprehensive, but because alternative investments show a low correlation with equities and bonds, which as we will see in part II reduces the overall risk of the portfolio, making them very attractive for diversification purposes.

Real Estate

Investing in land and buildings shows a low correlation with interest rates and stock markets, since market information is imperfect, each property is unique, liquidity is very scarce, and demand is affected by factors like demographics or availability of mortgage financing that are not necessarily correlated with bonds and equity markets.

---

[24] Interested readers can find further information on Hull (2000) or Jabbour and Budwick (2010).

[25] See Hull (2000), p. 644.

Commodities

Market participants can also invest in goods that are not perishable and that are the same anywhere no matter who produces it. These kind of goods are suitable to have a unique price, determined both for spot and derivatives markets. The most actively traded commodities are agricultural products (wheat, rice, soya, salt, sugar, coffee, ethanol...), all of them known as soft commodities, and mining products such as crude oil, coal, iron ore, aluminium, gold or silver—known as hard commodities.

Hedge Funds

As any other mutual funds, they are pools of private investment vehicles that allocate their assets in securities and derivatives. But through hedge funds investors try to obtain positive returns no matter if the stock market or the interest rates rise or fall, at the same time that they try to hedge risks using long and short positions.

Hedge funds can be highly leveraged—such that either the net long position can exceed 100% of the capital, or on the contrary they can have a net short position—and are characterized by an investment strategy that generally involves trading activities and a wide use of derivatives. Due to their low correlation with long-only assets, hedge funds show diversification benefits when included in a portfolio, but investors must be aware they have important disadvantages too. To illustrate, it depends on the fund manager ability to obtain excess returns, in order to obtain those excess returns they are usually not properly diversified, investors face high liquidity risk (usually withdrawals are restricted), they are usually registered only in tax havens and ultimately, in a word, they are suitable only for qualified investors with high income and investing only a small percentage of their personal wealth.

Five are most common hedge fund types[26]. First, relative value funds that use arbitrage and market neutral strategies and are often the least risky. Second, long/short funds that seek mispriced securities using either a fundamental or a quantitative approach to implement directional strategies. Third, global macro funds that analyze global macroeconomic events and implement derivative strategies to benefit from mispricing on currencies, stocks and bonds. Fourth, event driven funds that try to exploit pricing inefficiencies on corporate events such as mergers and distressed securities. Fifth, funds of hedge funds.

Private Equity and Venture Capital

Private equity refers to investments in non-publicly traded companies, and includes leveraged buyouts (LBOs), mezzanine financing, where investor buys preferred stock, and venture capital. Venture capital is financing for privately held companies in form of equity or convertible debt that are usually newborn or show high future potential growth. Venture capital investments are highly illiquid, requiring long investment periods to mature. Besides, since privately held companies are more difficult to value and future growth is based on

[26] For a nice and complete analysis on hedge funds, see López de Prado and Rodrigo-Illera (2005).

expectations, these investments are much riskier than average, so venture capitalist will require higher expected returns than in any other investments.

Part II: Financial Markets: The Investor's Point of View

In part I we have described financial markets as venues where economic agents look for financing. In such way, the classical taxonomy distinguishes between money markets (those which provide means of payment) and capital markets (those which provide long-term financing) at first level, whereas inside capital markets we differentiate between external financing (debt markets) and self financing (equities) on a second level. Both public and private agents issue securities and sell them to other market participants in exchange for the financing required. Finally, derivatives, alternative investments and currency markets account for other purposes, such as hedging risks, speculate or investing abroad.

However, we must realize that no financial markets would exist if there were no investors interested in buying such bonds, money assets, equities or derivatives. Financial markets offer a universe of investment alternatives to those agents, with excess savings available, seeking a combination of return and risk exposure that suits their profile. Thus, an investor facing all these alternatives would first wonder which forces guide financial markets, and after answering that question she would look for the investment procedures and allocation that better suit her objectives.

Once investment alternatives have been described in part I, now, in part II, we are going to examine how investors approach financial markets and which indicators they consider in their investment decisions. Besides, we will also provide a brief description of some study areas, such as portfolio management theory, asset pricing models, fundamental analysis, technical analysis, psychology of financial markets and behavioural finance which offer investment solutions that help market participants when facing their decision making process.

The layout of part II is as follows. We start by examining the concept and implications of market efficiency in chapter 6. In chapter 7 we analyse how investors should approach their investment setting and asset allocation decisions. Chapter 8 deals with two of the most important models in finance; namely, the modern portfolio theory (MPT) and the capital asset pricing model (CAPM). In chapter 9 we pay attention to stock analysis and the two generally used approaches: the technical analysis and the fundamental analysis. Lastly, chapter 10 is devoted to the insight on more recent theories that analyze 'real-world' markets where investors take cognitive and emotionally biased decisions.

Chapter 6

MARKET EFFICIENCY: RATIONAL EXPECTATIONS VS. ANIMAL SPIRITS

One of the roles financial markets play is to enhance the three basic characteristics of any financial asset investors must consider when they hold a security. Namely, liquidity, return and risk. The relationship among these three features—as it will be discussed below—is essential when making investment decisions, because the lower the liquidity and greater the risk of an asset, market participants will demand higher expected returns on their investments.

Liquidity measures the probability for an asset to be cashed out within a short period of time without a significant variation on its price. The rule is simple: the greater the liquidity of an asset the better for investors. On the other hand, return is the promise of a profit for providing savings to the market. Such promise could be determined in advance (in form of interest payments, as it happens with most money market instruments and fixed income assets) or not, in which case return comes in form of capital gains or losses. Finally, no matter whether an asset return is set in advance or not, investors will always face different sources of risk holding financial securities. Two of them come from the other basic features above—liquidity risk and market risk—, whereas other sources of uncertainty may come from the issuer's probability of default, the presence or not of collateral or other forms of insurance, etc.

Financial markets enhance those three asset characteristics above for several reasons. First, they improve liquidity since securities may be cashed out more easily and in shorter periods of time. Second, transparency and easy access for all market participants to every piece of information available is essential to reduce risks (and achieve efficiency, as we shall see next). And third, a large number of securities can be found that offer different risk-return profiles such that any investor may elaborate a portfolio that better suites her investment necessities.

But above all, financial markets will succeed in what Eugene Fama[1] defined as their primary role—to provide accurate signals for allocation of the economy's capital stock—if they are able to price securities in such a way that prices are a reliable indicator of the assets' fundamental or 'true' value. Such markets are said to be 'efficient', but the word 'efficiency'

[1] Fama (1970).

has different meanings. We shall not get confused here with similar concepts like, for example, 'economic efficiency', 'Pareto efficiency', 'business efficiency' and others. Economic efficiency means resources are used in such a way goods and services are produced at the lowest possible cost, but here we are not dealing with producing assets, just with pricing them. Pareto efficiency, on the other hand, applies to welfare comparison among individuals[2]. Finally, business efficiency relates to companies trying to minimize costs compared to earnings obtained (such as the *efficiency ratio* in banking).

In our context, competitive financial markets are allocate efficient since they distribute scarce resources between competing aims the most productive way. They also are operation efficient when transaction costs are determined competitively. Besides, if information provided is identical to all investors, a market is said to be information efficient in such a way that security prices instantaneously and fully adjust to all new information available. Then, a market is said to be perfectly efficient if it is simultaneously allocate, operation and information efficient[3].

As a consequence, we must understand efficient markets mean neither 'perfect' nor 'infallible' markets. A perfect market would be a fully competitive[4] market that provides all agents with complete and homogeneous information about the securities traded in them, in a context with no taxes, no transaction costs and no operative limits. Infallible markets, on the other hand, would imply a perfect ability to predict prices. But real-world markets are neither that perfect nor infallible, efficiency conditions are much less restrictive. An efficient market is not an unerring mechanism to prophesy future, it is an unbiased predictor of an asset's intrinsic value given information available. Financial markets will be efficient if prices fully reflect all information available at the market and adjust immediately to any new information being published. This postulate is known as the efficient market hypothesis (EMH) and is one of the most controversial assumptions in finance.

EMH implies present and future stock prices do not depend on past data, so market prices move randomly and investors cannot predict future movements based on historical series. Jensen[5] explains the EMH is in essence an extension of the zero profit competitive equilibrium condition to speculative markets under conditions of uncertainty. This way, a market would be efficient given the information available at the market if it is impossible to make economic profits by trading on the basis of such information. An efficient market would be, therefore, a *fair game* where all investors have the same possibilities to win or lose.

EMH was suggested by Eugene Fama (Fama, 1965, 1970), who divided it into three categories: the weak-form, the semistrong-form and the strong-form of efficient market hypothesis. Under the weak-form EMH, current stock prices fully reflect all currently available market information. Hence, past price, volume and any other historical information would have no relationship with the future direction of security prices, so technical analysis[6] is helpless. Under the assumption of semistrong-form EMH, current stock prices rapidly adjust to the release of any market and non-market information available to the agents. In this

[2] Named after Vilfredo Pareto, an Italian economist. Given an allocation of goods among individuals, a change is considered a 'Pareto improvement' only if at least one individual improves without making any other be worse, so a set of goods is said to be Pareto efficient if a Pareto improvement is not feasible

[3] Blake (2000).

[4] No participant with market power to set prices, no barriers to entry or exit and equal access to production technology.

[5] Jensen (1978).

[6] We shall have an insight on technical analysis in section 9.1.

case, investors cannot achieve excess returns using fundamental analysis[7]. Finally, the strong-form EMH version implies that prices fully reflect all public and private information. In other words, the strong-form EMH assumes markets where information is cost-free and available to all market participants at the same time.

Statistical tests for correlation can be implemented in order to determine whether a market is efficient or not. Most market improvements the last two decades were set with the objective of enhancing transparency, speed of information dissemination, competitiveness, and effective allocation. Still, some evidence against the EMH can be found, such as calendar effects, small cap effects, value shares outperforming growth shares, dividend yield effects, and others. Hence, one essential question arises: Which forces guide financial markets behaviour?

Academic finance is split in two tendencies, according to the emphasis they put on the two forces that are behind financial markets: rational expectations and animal spirits. The EMH states all market participants adopt rational investment decisions using all available information, and one may assume this holds most of the time. Nevertheless, information is vast, endless and rarely cost-free, so it is not much saying that analysts, through fundamental research and careful interpretation of data, can obtain further understanding on stock prices and future company performance. Besides, behavioural finance argues that market evidence shows prices are determined by agents on the market (not only private investors, but brokers, dealers and professional fund managers, too) with biased expectations, who exhibit loss aversion instead of risk aversion, and tend to evaluate investments on an individual asset basis rather than from a portfolio diversification perspective.

Interestingly, Statman (1999) highlights the term 'market efficiency' has actually two meanings: one is that investors cannot systematically beat the market, the other is that security prices are rational, meaning they reflect only fundamental characteristics, such as risk, but not psychological, such as sentiment. In words of Statman, *finance scholars and professionals would do well to accept market efficiency in the beat-the-market sense but reject in the rational-prices sense*[8]. This would allow finance researchers to stop fighting the 'market efficiency battle', and start exploring asset-pricing models that reflect both psychological and fundamental characteristics.

Therefore, in the following chapters we are going to describe some of the most essential areas of investment analysis and decision making we can find on theory of finance, and for a better understanding we are going to do it differentiating those based on rational expectations and those that work if EMH does not hold. In chapters 7 and 8 we shall describe how investors, based on rational expectations, would approach their investment setting, price securities on the market and manage their portfolios. Next, in chapters 9 and 10 we offer a brief description of the basics of technical analysis, fundamental analysis and behavioural finance—investment theories that are only useful if EMH does not hold.

---

[7] Fundamental analysis is to be described in section 9.2

[8] Statman (1999), p. 18.

Chapter 7

INVESTING IN FINANCIAL MARKETS

"Markets can remain irrational far longer than you can remain solvent"

John M. Keynes

Investors should not just consider a particular security and decide whether to invest in it or not. It is not that straightforward, since investment decisions depend on much more variables than those derived from buying a specific asset. All agents have particular objectives about what they expect to get from their savings when invested in financial markets, and they must be aware they face some constraints, too.

In this section we are going to examine how investors should approach their investment setting and their asset allocation decision, and that analysis will lead us to one crucial finding: investors' preferences exhibit a risk-return trade-off that were determinant for the development of the modern portfolio theory.

7.1. INVESTMENT SETTING AND THE ASSET ALLOCATION DECISION

Investors build up portfolios, i.e. a collection of financial assets, with the purpose of protecting their savings from inflation by investing them in such a way they earn an acceptable combination of the three basic characteristics of financial assets—risk, return and liquidity. But in order to do that, individual investors must first consider which stage of the investment life cycle they are at[1]. People make financial plans according to their age, personal income (both present and expected in the future), financial status and needs. Hence, before investing an agent must set aside funds for what she expects it will be her basic needs considering her whole life.

'Investment life cycle' classical definition considers four stages: accumulation, consolidation, spending and gifting. The accumulation phase covers from early to middle working years, when investors have a long time horizon and growing earnings capacity. This stage is characterized by a higher risk appetite: immediate needs are satisfied, and—since

[1] For a detailed analysis on theoretical background for this assertion, see Antelo and Peón (2011).

they expect higher earnings over a long period of time in the future—people tend to do long-term plans, increasing risks hoping to obtain above average returns to achieve them. The second stage is the consolidation stage, when investors still have a long time horizon and earnings largely exceed needs, but they have already accumulated some assets so they start to be concerned about protecting their wealth from inflation and unnecessary risks. People at this stage tend to prefer moderate risk investments. The third stage is the spending phase that begins with retirement. Now, earnings exhibit a significant drop, with basic needs usually exceeding them. Besides, time horizon has shortened, so investment goals at this stage are liquidity, low risk investments and protection against inflation. Finally, the gifting stage is the one where the investor faces a similar situation to that on the spending phase, but at this point she starts planning her heritage, so tax minimization activities become more relevant.

This schedule applies not only individual investors. Institutional investors, such as mutual funds, pension funds, insurance companies, banks and financial institutions, must consider their objectives and constraints before investing, too. Insurance companies, for example, are subject to the 'prudent expert' rule, while banks main concern is to generate returns in excess of their costs of funding over short periods of time, due to their high liquidity needs. Pension funds, on the other hand, have long time horizons and low liquidity needs, and are only limited by their specific regulation, whereas mutual funds must comply both with their specific guidelines and the risk profile and investment choices required by investors on the prospectus.

Therefore, the first thing any investor should do is to identify her objectives and constraints. Objectives are basically getting the maximum return assuming the least possible risks, since rational investors are risk averse. Risk tolerance, as we saw, depends on personal factors such as age, stage on the life cycle, personal preferences and existing wealth. Return objectives, on the other hand, include interests, capital gains, income needs and capital preservation. Investors must be aware that, many times, required returns do not fulfil their desired returns, and that both could even be unrealistic given market conditions.

By constraints we mean the basic limits investors face; namely, liquidity needs, time horizon, fiscal environment, and legal requirements. The first restriction—liquidity needs—is binding because unplanned necessity for cash may involve selling assets at disadvantaged conditions. Hence, investors must hold part of their wealth in cash and other liquid investments that allow them to fund planned or unexpected situations that may arise. Regarding the time horizon, most investments do not yield returns immediately, or at least, investors should not expect that. People with shorter time horizons should engage in low risk investments, while assets like equity or real estate, for example, require longer periods of time to mature. Likewise, the fiscal environment reflects the fact that different tax treatments may apply to income and capital gains, mutual funds or other investment vehicles. Besides, investors must consider there is a trade-off between taxes and diversification needs, because buying or selling a stock in order to diversify a portfolio implies transaction costs and taxes on capital gains. Finally, legal requirements stand for any other regulations that could be applied.

Three-stage investor's strategy:

- Asset allocation
- Security selection
- Market timing

Once goals and limits have been determined, investors construct their strategy, based on three broad decisions: asset allocation (which asset classes are to be included and in which proportion), security selection (choosing the individual assets of the portfolio) and market timing (deciding when to buy or sell those securities).

Asset allocation is, by far, the most important of the three. The purpose of asset allocation is to determine the mix of assets in the portfolio that better suits risk, return and liquidity preferences of each particular investor. The lower the liquidity and greater the risk of an asset, market participants will demand higher expected returns. With that idea in their minds, market participants should first analyze all different existing investment opportunities. That is, they should consider investing in the five basic families of assets we have seen in part I of the book, according to their properties and expected performance available: namely, cash and other money assets, government bonds, corporate bonds, equities, and other alternative investments. They could even go a step further, differentiating for example between investment grade and high yield bonds (being the latter riskier bonds that are more correlated with the stock market performance), convertible bonds (which could be considered sort of a mix of equity and fixed income securities), smallcap and bluechip stocks (which tend to exhibit different performance across the economic cycle), growth versus value investing, foreign currencies or different alternative investments such as real estate, soft and hard commodities, etc.

Once investors face a comprehensive list of investments available, the purpose of asset allocation will be to determine the mix of assets in the portfolio that better suits risk, return and liquidity preferences of each particular investor. Those preferences and the stage of the life cycle she is at, together with market and economic conditions, will then determine how much of each asset class should the investor hold in her portfolio. Portfolios are selected to be neutral, over-weighted or under-weighted in each of those five asset classes depending on the stage of the economic cycle we are at that moment, particularly according to the GDP growth rate, the inflation rate and the interest rates. In any case, investors should consider investing at any time in all the five basic categories outlined above. This is because these families tend to exhibit a low correlation among them, which as we shall see later in this section reduces overall risk of the portfolio due to diversification benefits.

Finally, any portfolio should be diversified at two levels: between asset categories and within asset categories. Therefore, after the asset allocation is determined, investors try to identify investments in segments of each asset category that may perform differently under different market conditions, picking up those expected to outperform. Whether each particular security is found to be overpriced or underpriced through fundamental analysis will determine their selection for the portfolio, whereas market timing mostly depends on technical analysis.

Theory of finance argues that rational investor's decisions may be explained as agents featuring utility functions (see figure 23 below) with a set of indifference curves, where—since risk and return are the main goals to achieve—each curve represent different combinations of risk and return that provide the same level of utility. Investors have a required rate of return for every investment, where such rate depends on the nominal risk free rate and the risk premium demanded to that security in reward of the risk being assumed. Mathematically, it can be stated as

Required rate = (1+Real rate)·(1+Expected inflation rate)·(1+Risk premium) – 1. (25)

Then, they compare that required rate on every asset with the return expected on them, given their price and market conditions at any time. Only combinations of assets with an expected return that meets the required rate given their risk premium will be considered.

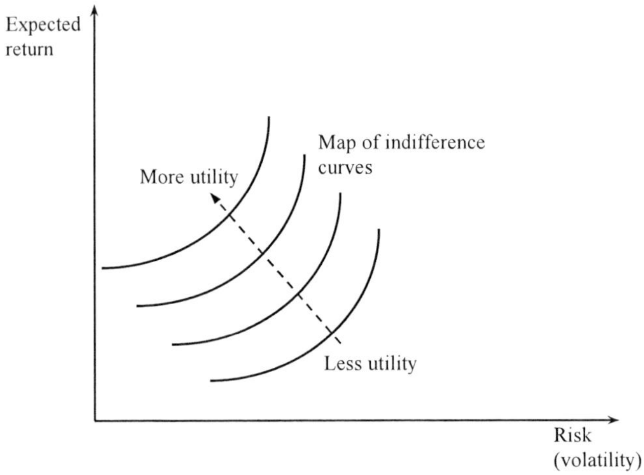

Figure 23. Investor's utility function.

In addition, we also need a useful measure for risk. Since investors interpret risk as the variability of potential outcomes around the expected return of an asset, variance (the average squared deviation of returns around the expected return) and standard deviation (calculated as the square root of variance, which allows volatility to be measured in the same units as return) are the most common ways to quantify risk. Further on, on next chapter, we will describe the capital asset pricing model (CAPM), where we will see that only a portion of a security's risk—called systematic risk—matters for asset pricing purposes. A new measure (the so-called *beta*) will arise as a quantification of systematic risk. But so far, we will consider volatility for this purpose.

Investors want to maximize their returns for a given level of risk. Since indifference curves in the (expected risk, expected return)-space do not intersect, investors would want to be on the highest possible indifference curve. Besides, rational investors are risk averse. This implies a positive relationship between expected returns and expected risk. Highly risk-averse investors will feature very steep indifference curves, whereas flat curves indicate higher tolerance for risk. Investors will then try to implement an asset allocation that maximizes their level of expected utility, given market conditions and their personal constraints (liquidity needs, time horizon, etc.). But how would we do that?

7.2. Risk-Return Trade-off

Indifference curves like those above depicted are representative of investors that prefer higher returns to lower returns for a given risk level, and prefer to assume less risk to more risk in order to achieve a given level of return. Hence, there exists a risk-return trade-off on investor's preferences. But on the market there is a risk-return trade-off among assets too: in order to achieve higher expected returns, investors must put their money on assets with a higher possibility of loss, since risk is the chance that an investment's actual return will be different than expected. The contrary would be nonsense. Imagine an asset that exhibits a lower expected return than other, with both securities having the same expected risk: clearly all investors will prefer to buy the second one. The same happens when comparing assets with the same expected return but different levels of risk, where investors will prefer the less risky security. Therefore, investors must understand making money at financial markets never comes at no risk. Given risk-return trade-off, investor's objective should always be maximizing her risk-adjusted return.

Example 12

Given two assets, A and B, let's consider asset A shows a higher expected return assuming a higher expected risk than B. In this situation, none of them would be preferred[2] compared to the other, because we could not move from one asset to the other without either decreasing return or increasing risk. Then, choosing either A or B will depend on the investor's preference for risk and return, that is, her utility function represented by the set of indifference curves. We must be aware that in such case two investors with different utility functions may prefer to choose different assets.

Or not, because there is a third possibility. Consider a third asset, C, which is actually a portfolio combining 50% invested on asset A and 50% invested on asset B. It can be shown mathematically that the expected return on asset C is equal to the mean of assets A and B expected returns. But, on the contrary, the risk (measured as the standard deviation of returns) of such portfolio is usually lower than the mean of assets A and B expected risks!

This is so because returns on the individual securities may vary in different directions one from each other, reducing the aggregate variability of the portfolio C. The way two assets move compared to each other is measured by their correlation coefficient (a measure of the covariance of returns of both assets compared to their individual variances that has no units, varying from −1 to 1). A correlation coefficient of 1 means returns move always together in the same direction, such that both assets are perfectly correlated and there are not diversification benefits. On the other hand, a coefficient of −1 implies assets are perfectly negatively correlated, whereas as correlation gets closer to 0, we say those two assets are uncorrelated.

Correlation is the engine that drives the whole theory of portfolio diversification we shall see next. Combining assets with low correlations, investors can build portfolios—like our asset C in figure 24—that maximize their utility function compared to the utility they could achieve if they invest just in a single security. That is also the reason why asset allocation is so important. Assets inside any of the five categories we have seen in part I[3] tend to have high

---

[2] Think here of preference in an approach similar to efficiency in the Pareto sense. An asset would be said to dominate another if it yields a higher return assuming no more expected risk, or if it conveys a lower risk for at least the same expected return.

[3] Namely, cash and other money assets, government bonds, corporate bonds, equities, and alternative investments.

correlations—the closer to one, the worst—such that a combination of two assets A and B would fall in between (see the continuous line in figure 25).

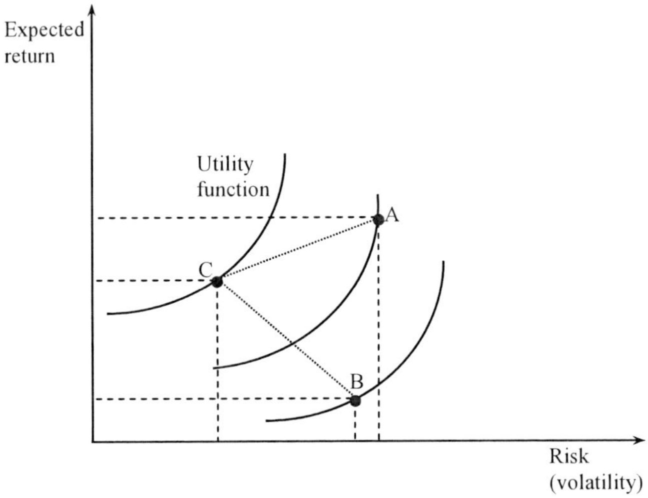

Figure 24. Combining assets to achieve higher levels of utility.

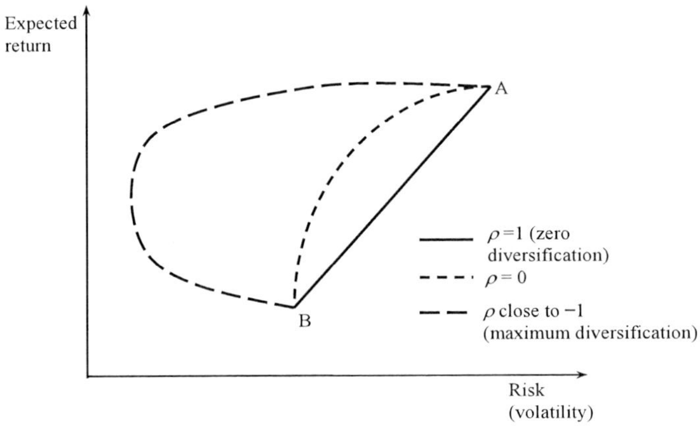

Figure 25. Degrees of correlation and diversification.

On the contrary, assets across different families tend to exhibit lower correlation levels among them in such a way that a combination of two assets A and B would yield a portfolio with an average expected return, but a lower risk (see the dotted and the dashed lines in figure 25 above).

Chapter 8

PORTFOLIO MANAGEMENT AND ASSET PRICING MODELS

Following we are going to have an insight on two of the most important theories in finance: modern portfolio theory and the capital asset pricing model. The first was essential to understand the benefits of diversification, while the second provided the first widely used approach to price risky assets. As any other theory both have significant shortcomings, but it was their straightforward but also brilliant analysis that led to relevant conclusions on essential topics like risk and return, diversification, systematic versus unsystematic risk and required return what made these theories still widely used today, nearly sixty years after their release.

8.1. MODERN PORTFOLIO THEORY

In 1952, based on the risk-return trade-off properties and the benefits of diversification shown in previous section, Harry Markowitz (Markowitz, 1952) wrote one of the most acclaimed works in finance, developing the basics of the modern portfolio theory (MPT). Further improvements by James Tobin (1958), Jack Treynor (1961, 1965), William Sharpe (1963, 1964), John Lintner (1965) and Jan Mossin (1966) set not only the bulk of MPT but of the asset pricing models (APM) too, as we will see on the following subsection.

Markowitz (1952)'s model set investor's behaviour in terms of risk and return, introducing diversification as an essential way to reduce risk. His main contribution was to explicitly express what the rational behaviour of any investor should be: trying to build portfolios that maximize the expected return for a given level of risk, or alternatively, that minimized risk exposure for a given level of required expected return. This is so because two opposite forces drive investors' behaviour: the desirability of higher earnings, and the dissatisfaction produced by the higher risk that necessarily has to be assumed in order to aspire to higher profits.

This way, Markowitz worked out a mathematical model where, given a set of securities with different expected risks and returns, the expected mean return of every feasible portfolio was maximized for a given risk level, or either risk was minimized for an expected mean return. Due to correlation diversification properties, different asset combinations could provide portfolios that are efficient when compared with the securities alone. This optimal set of portfolios is called the efficient frontier, which provides the highest return at each level of risk. It can be illustrated as follows.

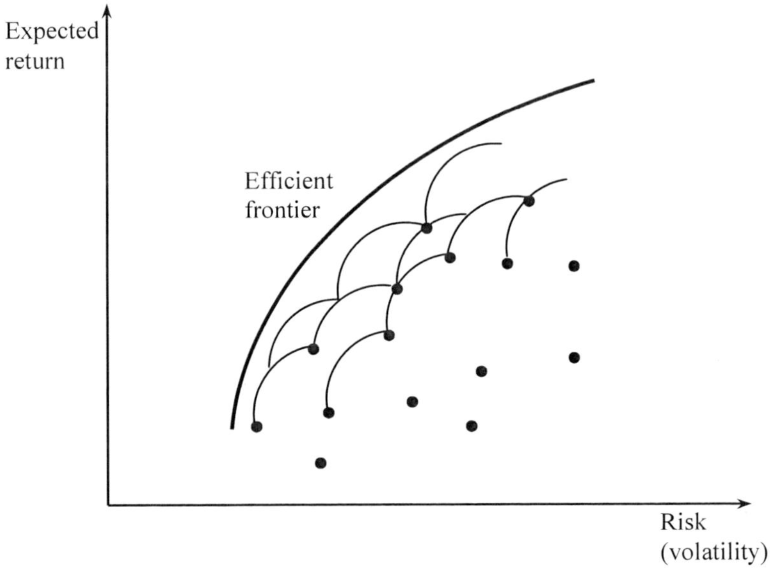

Figure 26. The Markowitz efficient frontier.

Each point in the graph represents an asset (depicted as a combination of its expected risk and return). Each line between any two assets gives the achievable combinations between them, given their correlation coefficient, as we saw in figures 24 and 25 in chapter 7. And 'combining all possible combinations' (i.e. using all assets with the correlations among them) to calculate the best possible combination gives us the efficient frontier. It determines the objective market opportunities, so it is unique to all investors because we are assuming markets are efficient and agents have all the same information. Knowing this, every investor will face her indifference curves against the efficient frontier, selecting the portfolio that maximizes her risk-adjusted return (which graphically accounts for the point where the efficient frontier is tangent to the highest possible indifference curve, see figure 27). Obviously, two investors with different utility functions will choose two different combinations, but in any case both portfolios will be on the efficient frontier, since this line provides the combinations with the best risk-adjusted properties.

Markowitz (1952)'s model has an important handicap. Though we have not seen the mathematics behind the model, readers should be aware that—in order to maximize expected returns on all feasible portfolios for every given level of risk—we need to calculate a huge number of mean returns, variances and covariances between assets. Just as an example, if you wanted to draw the efficient frontier on the S&P500 index, you will need to estimate more than 125,000 variables. Simply unfeasible!

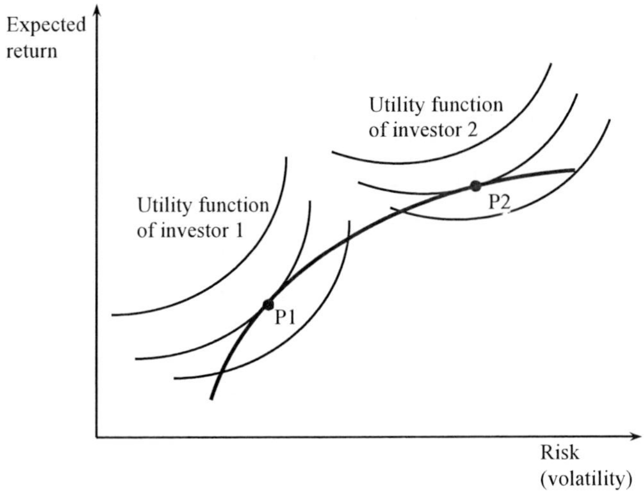

Figure 27. Selecting optimal portfolios.

William Sharpe (Sharpe, 1963) avoided this problem assuming that the statistical dependence between the returns of two assets is not direct, but derived from the relationship between the return on those assets and a relevant market index. That is, instead of considering the correlation between any two assets in the portfolio, the relevant correlation we should estimate is the one existing between any single security and the index for that market. This way, the return on any asset i at any given time t could be expressed as an equation on the index expected return, as follows:

$$R_{it} = \alpha + \beta \cdot R_{it} + \varepsilon_t, \qquad (26)$$

where R_{it} is the return on asset i at any moment t, α is a constant that gives the return on the asset that is independent on the return of the market index, β is a measure of the sensitivity of the asset return when the market index moves, R_{mt} is the return on the market index at that moment t, and ε_t is a random variable. This way, only parameters α and β, as well as the mean and variance on the market index are needed to draw Markowitz efficient frontier. Calculation of the expected return and risk of every asset i affords

$$\mathbf{E}[R_{it}] = \alpha + \beta \cdot \mathbf{E}[R_m], \qquad (27)$$

$$\mathbf{Var}[R_i] = \beta^2 \cdot \mathbf{Var}[R_m] + \mathbf{Var}[\varepsilon], \qquad (28)$$

where operators $\mathbf{E}[\cdot]$ and $\mathbf{Var}[\cdot]$ stand for expected return and variance of such return, respectively. Doing the same for any feasible portfolio, we can see a security or portfolio risk could be divided in two terms, as follows:

$$\text{Total risk} = \text{Systematic risk} + \text{Unsystematic risk}. \qquad (29)$$

On one hand, systematic risk, which depends on β and the market risk, represents changes in the economy that are not directly related to the security and cannot be diversified. On the other hand, unsystematic risk measures the specific risk of the asset that can be diversified away when we build a portfolio, by adding more and more assets to it as we can see in figure 28.

This way, Sharpe solved the investor's decision process the same way as Markowitz did, solving a mathematical optimization program where risk was minimized for an expected mean return, but instead of using data of risk, return and correlation among securities, he used as inputs the equation (26) for each asset. Estimations required to draw the efficient frontier were largely reduced[1], and the selection of each investor's optimal portfolio would be done the same way, by facing indifference curves against the efficient frontier and selecting the tangent point.

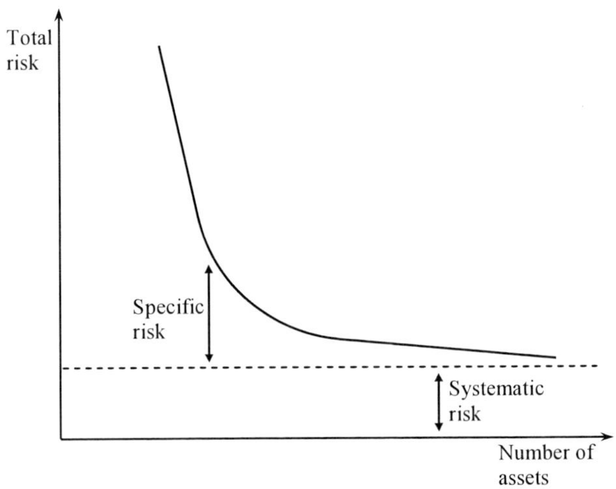

Figure 28. Risk diversification vs. assets in a portfolio.

All these concepts by Sharpe, namely the difference between systematic and unsystematic risk, and the idea that unsystematic risk could be diversified away, were essential for Sharpe (1963), Treynor (1965), Lintner (1965) and Mossin (1966) to derive the Capital Asset Pricing Model.

8.2. Asset Pricing Models

According with Markowitz (1952)'s model, investors face a risk-return trade-off on their investment decisions. They will select assets or portfolios that are efficient in terms of risk and expected return, and securities that are not competitive—either because they offer a low expected return assuming the same risk, or because they are too risky for the expected return they offer—will not be attractive. Besides, according to William Sharpe (Sharpe, 1963), risk

[1] Following our example, estimations required to draw the efficient frontier on the S&P500 index, would be reduced from 125,000 to about 1,500 variables.

could be expressed in terms of sensitivity against the market index instead of volatility. Such risk could be split in two terms: systematic risk (unavoidable) and unsystematic risk, which is specific to that security and could be diversified away combining it in a portfolio.

Using these two models, we could determine which asset prices clear markets so they are in equilibrium. Assets offering a low expected return for their risk level would be overpriced, so market forces would lower its price, and the opposite would happen for under-priced assets. But which measure of risk should be considered for pricing purposes? We know that combining assets in portfolios some risk (unsystematic risk) could be diversified away. Therefore, only systematic risk should be taken into account to determine whether an asset is properly priced or not. Capital asset pricing model (CAPM) was developed independently by Sharpe, Treynor, Lintner and Mossin applying those concepts above by Markowitz, Tobin and Sharpe himself. It provides a mathematical model to determine an equilibrium relationship between the risk of an asset (or a portfolio of assets) and the return it offers.

James Tobin (Tobin, 1958), independently to Markowitz's work on portfolio theory, analyzed the Keynesian theory on liquidity preference—an inverse relationship between the demand for cash balances and the rate of interest. Economic agents tend to hold some proportion of their portfolios in cash—which could be thought of as 'non-interest bearing government bonds', yielding no return—instead of investing in interest bearing government bonds. Further than that, Tobin not only tries to explain the existence of a demand for cash, but the rationale for a demand that shows an inverse relationship with the differential in yields between government bonds and cash. In Tobin's analysis, an agent's decision will depend on her preferences, the expected return on the bonds, and risk, measured as the possibility of her portfolio to exhibit losses.

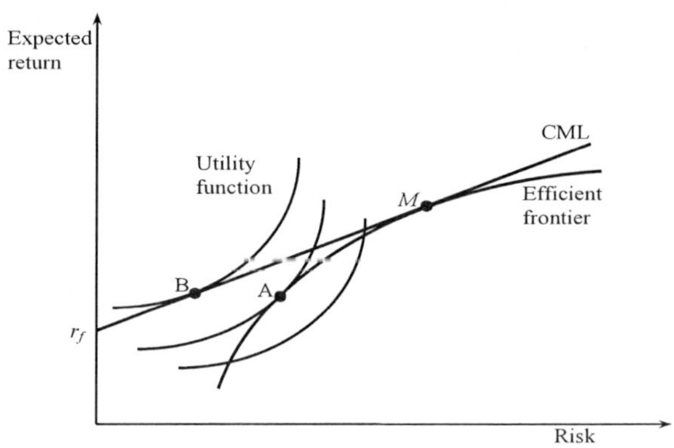

Figure 29. The capital market line (CML).

Sharpe used Tobin's ideas to extend Markowitz's model including a risk-free asset, offering a risk-free return, r_f, at which market participants could both either invest their savings or borrow money to invest it in risky assets[2]. He showed that, through this

[2] Extended versions of this model would consider a more realistic situation where the cost of borrow is higher than the return on the risk-free asset.

combination of risky and risk-free assets, investors could reach higher utility levels than investing in the efficient frontier alone. This can be illustrated as in figure 29 above.

Considering only the efficient frontier of risky assets, our investor selected portfolio A that maximized her utility function. But when introducing the possibility of investing (or borrowing) at a risk-free rate r_f, she could increase her utility selecting portfolio B, which is a linear combination of the risk-free asset and the market portfolio, *M*. Tobin's separation theorem states that market portfolio *M* is independent from the utility function of any investor. Utility functions determine which amount is borrowed or invested at the risk-free rate, but do not determine which optimal portfolio is to be combined with the riskless asset. This is so because such portfolio is the one that dominates all the other available portfolios when combined with the risk-free asset, and is determined by market opportunities regardless the utility function of investors and their attitude toward risk.

The introduction of a riskless asset changes the Markowitz efficient frontier—depicted in figure 26—into a straight line, as given by r_fM. This line dominates all portfolios in terms of return offered for the level of risk assumed, and is called the Capital Market Line (CML), which equation is given by

$$\mathbf{E}[R_p] = r_f + \frac{\mathbf{E}[R_m] - r_f}{\sigma_m} \cdot \sigma_p , \tag{30}$$

where $\mathbf{E}[R_p]$ and $\mathbf{E}[R_m]$ are the expected return on a given portfolio p and on the market portfolio M, respectively, r_f is the return on the risk-free asset, and σ_p and σ_m are the standard deviations[3] of portfolio and market portfolio returns, respectively.

The CML provides a description of a capital market in equilibrium: under this model the only risky asset purchased is portfolio *M*—called the market portfolio because it contains all risky assets in existence as stocks, bonds and others, so it represents the completely diversified portfolio[4]—which is to be combined with the risk-free asset. Investors' only decision is to determine which combination of risk and return better suits them, varying the proportion of their investment in the risky portfolio *M* and the risk-free asset, according to their individual preferences.

Portfolios on the CML are efficient... and easy to find. Sharpe ratio measures the risk premium any asset provides compared to the risk an investor is exposed to when investing in it:

$$S_p = \frac{\mathbf{E}[R_m] - r_f}{\sigma_p} . \tag{31}$$

Besides, Sharpe ratio of efficient portfolios would be the same as the slope of the CML, so it is easy to see portfolios on the CML are efficient compared to any other assets below the line, because their Sharpe ratio is higher. We shall better see it through an example.

[3] Another measure for risk, standard deviation accounts for the square root of variance.

[4] Anyway, you do not need to buy all securities in the market to reach a completely diversified portfolio. As suggested by figure 28, indicating that specific risk decreases as the number of assets on portfolio increases, studies have shown unsystematic risk is mostly diversified away when assets in a portfolio are about 30 and above. See, for example, Elton et al. (1977) or Statman (1987)

Example 13

In a market where we can obtain a 1% return at no risk, we are given the expected return and risk (measured as standard deviation of returns) on two risky portfolios, P and M—both lying on the efficient frontier—and one risky security, X:

	$\mathbf{E}[R_p]$	σ_p
P	3.50%	4.40%
$\boldsymbol{M}$	**4.50%**	**4.60%**
X	4.00%	7.00%

Finding which asset would be preferable in terms of return over risk assumed would be as simple as calculating their Sharpe ratio. For example, for portfolio P it would account as

$$S_p = \frac{\mathbf{E}[R_p] - r_f}{\sigma_p} = \frac{0.035 - 0.01}{0.044} = 0.7955.$$

Doing the same for portfolio M and security X we would have

	$\mathbf{E}[R_p]$	σ_p	S_p
P	3.50%	4.40%	0.7955
$\boldsymbol{M}$	**4.50%**	**4.60%**	**0.9780**
X	4.00%	7.00%	0.5714

and both Sharpe ratios and the CML can be illustrated as follows.

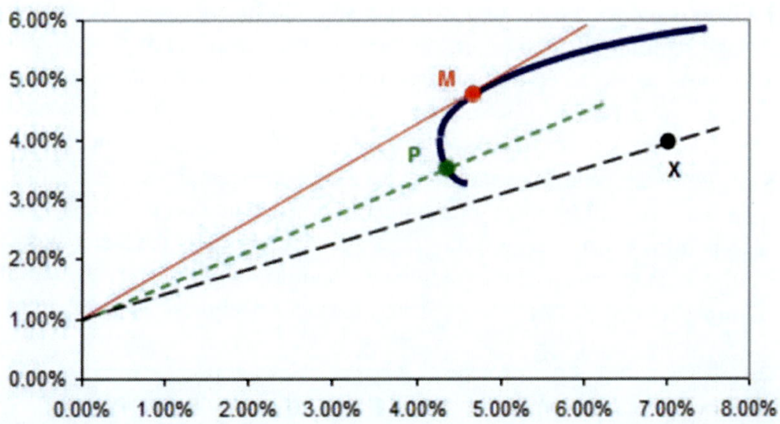

Figure 30. Sharpe ratios and the CML.

Portfolio M has the highest Sharpe ratio and, as we can see graphically in figure 30, the combination of the riskless asset with portfolio M results in the highest possible line available (since point M would be tangent with the line at that point). That line would be the CML, as we have seen, which yields the highest possible Sharpe ratio.

This analysis is also helpful to provide a means to price financial assets. CAPM model shows investors can put their money in a portfolio that completely diversifies unsystematic risk away. But anyway, instead of buying the whole market portfolio, an investor may consider to buy just a particular security. She will evaluate the expected return and the asset's total risk as we saw before, but she could as well use CAPM principles to price such asset. Since unsystematic risk could be diluted through diversification, she will be compensated only for the systematic risk she assumes. Given the CML equation and rearranging, we have

$$\mathbf{E}[R_p] = r_f + (\mathbf{E}[R_m] - r_f) \cdot \beta_p, \quad (32)$$

where $\beta_p = \sigma_p / \sigma_m$ measures the sensitivity of an efficient portfolio p to movements in market portfolio returns. Similarly, this equation could be applied to any single security i, providing a means to price assets and portfolios, whether efficient or not:

$$\mathbf{E}[R_i] = r_f + (\mathbf{E}[R_m] - r_f) \cdot \beta_i, \quad (33)$$

where $\beta_i = \sigma_{im} / \sigma_m^2$ [5] measures the sensitivity of the asset i to movements in market portfolio returns. Equation (33) is the equation of a line, the so-called security market line (SML), and represents the core of the CAPM: the expected return of any asset i should equal the return on the riskless asset, plus the market risk premium multiplied by the asset's systematic risk (measured by its beta coefficient).

Plotting the expected return of security i, $\mathbf{E}[R_i]$, stated in (33), against the beta coefficient, $\beta_i = \sigma_{im} / \sigma_m^2$, we can obtain the SML, as depicted in figure 31 below.

This way, we can see it clear any asset with a systematic risk—measured by the beta coefficient—higher than average[6] should yield a higher expected return. For example, an asset with a beta equal to 2 should be expected to yield (using the SML equation) two times the market risk premium plus the return on the risk-free asset, r_f, whereas an asset with a beta equal to 0.5 should be expected to yield half the market risk premium plus r_f. Securities with beta higher than one are said to be 'aggressive', because they exhibit higher risk and higher expected return, whereas those with beta lower than one are said to be 'defensive'.

The SML gives the return we should expect an asset should yield if CAPM holds. But it could happen we had a different prediction using other valuation methods. This makes SML equation also helpful because it provides a rule to determine which securities on the market we expect to be underpriced and which ones overpriced. Assets with combination beta-expected return above the SML are expected to yield a highest return than determined by

[5] A rather technical sidelight: though apparently different, β_p and β_i equations stated here are in fact the same. Furthermore, they provide further insight in what CML equation means. Beta coefficient measures the covariance between an asset and the market portfolio, σ_{im}, divided by the variance of market portfolio. But for efficient portfolios (lying on the CML line) it can be proved mathematically beta could be calculated as volatility on the portfolio, σ_p, divided by volatility on the market portfolio, σ_m. This is so because efficient portfolios exhibit a correlation equal to one with market portfolio. That is, investing in those portfolios there is no risk that could be further diversified.

[6] That is, higher than the systematic risk of the market portfolio, which by definition equals one.

CAPM, so they are underpriced; and vice versa, assets below the SML are expected to yield a lower return than determined by CAPM, so they are overpriced. Again, we shall see it clearer through an example.

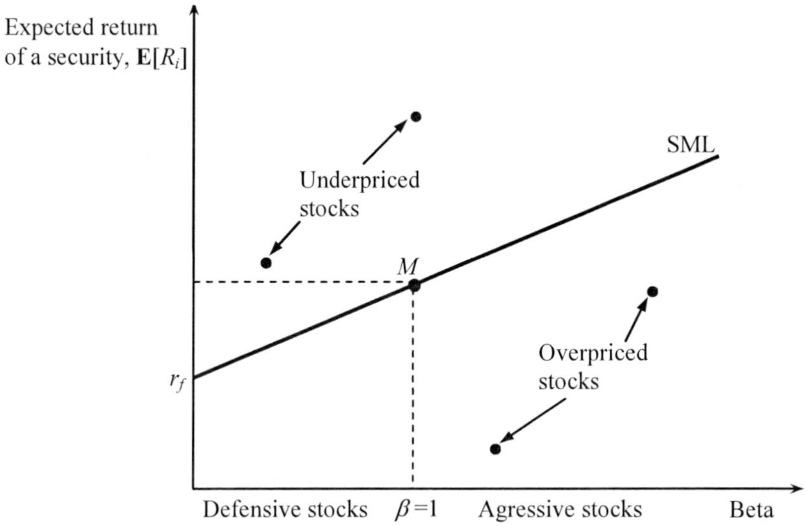

Figure 31. The security market line (SML).

Example 14

Using CAPM, and given market conditions (market portfolio is expected to yield an annual return of 10%, a risk-free asset is available and yields 2% per annum) we determine a stock A should yield an expected return given by the SML equation $\mathbf{E}[R_A] = 0.02 + 0.08 \cdot \beta_A$. The beta of this stock has been previously calculated and it is equal to 1.5. This way, using CAPM we know the expected return asset A should yield is $0.02 + 0.08 \cdot 1.15 = 0.14$, i.e. 14%.

On the other hand, we are given the price of one share of A today is $10, and it is expected to pay a dividend over the next year of $1. We have read several analyst recommendations saying the expected price of the stock over the next year is $11. Can we say the price of the stock today ($10) is too high (meaning the stock is overpriced) or too low (meaning it is underpriced)?

We can if we use CAPM. First, we calculate the expected return this asset would yield if it paid $1 in dividends and its price would actually rise from $10 to $11. Such return amounts to $\mathbf{E}[R_A]$ = [$1+($11–S10)]/$10 = 20%. Therefore, asset A is expected to yield 20%, and when using CAPM we would say an asset with beta coefficient equal to 1,5 should yield 14%. Graphically:

Stock A is underpriced today because, in order to yield through dividends and expected price increase the same as it is expected using CAPM, the value of share A today should be higher[7].

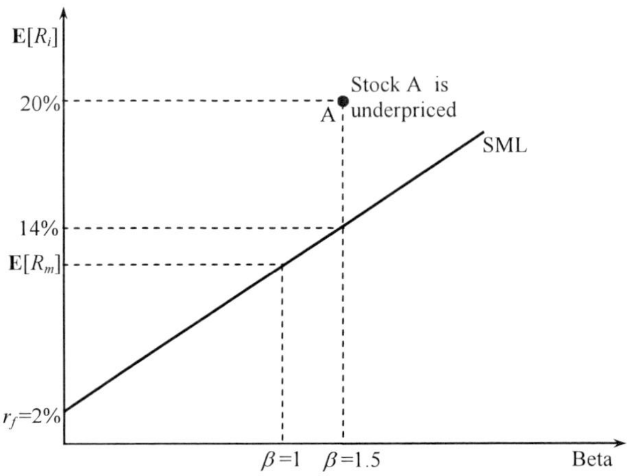

Figure 32. Plotting an underpriced stock.

Shortcomings on Markowitz and CAPM Models

Though MPT and CAPM are two of the most acclaimed models and they are still widely used today, some shortcomings are in order. First, their initial assumptions are unrealistic to some extent. Assumptions like using the same rate for borrowing and lending, normal distribution of returns, introducing it as a just one-period game, or pretending there are no taxes, transaction costs or inflation in the economy were solved lately in extended versions, but others are hardly observable in real world. This implies we should take findings of these models in a looser way.

Second, the lack of realism in statistical assumptions is severe and even more problematic than that of the above-mentioned assumptions. Both models assume all investors expect the same probability distributions of future returns for all assets in the market (called homogeneous expectations assumption). Ask ten people in a room about what their expectations over the next year on risk and return of securities in the Dow Jones index, and you will find anything but a homogeneous answer. Furthermore, the models assume investors' beliefs match the true distribution of returns, or equivalently, that investors have not biased expectations. Had they, market prices would be information inefficient. On the contrary, behavioural finance (a topic we will see later on) considers models were agents exhibit overconfidence and biased expectations. Finally, another statistical assumption of MPT and CAPM theories we might question is the adoption of variance of returns as an adequate measure of risk, when actually risk is asymmetric in nature: we are only concerned with the probability of losing, not with the probability of earning higher returns than the average.

[7] We could calculate it should be approximately equal to \$10.526, because in that case the expected return of asset A would be (\$1+\$0.526)/\$10.526=14%, as predicted by CAPM.

CAPM was based on Sharpe ideas to solve Markowitz MPT problems to estimate so many variables. CAPM considers that the relevant correlation we should estimate is the one existing between any single security and an index for that market, but Sharpe actually proposed a multiple index model where stocks could be affected by more than one index (stock market index, GDP growth, inflation rate, etc.), which seems to be much more realistic. Moreover, market portfolio is not observable. It should consist of all assets in all markets (including real estate, art, human capital...), so in practice researchers use a market index as a proxy for the true market portfolio. This makes CAPM not empirically testable, like the Roll (1977)'s critique shown.

As an alternative to the two last drawbacks, a new theory was set: the arbitrage pricing theory (APT). This model, offered by Stephen Ross[8], likewise CAPM is an equilibrium model (in fact, it considers conditions at which the market would be in equilibrium because assets are correctly priced), but with several differences with respect to CAPM. Among them, APT considers asset returns are explained by sensitivity to other factors aside the market index, like interest rates, GDP growth, inflation rate, etc. More relevant, APT is not based on searching efficient portfolios as CAPM, but it uses an arbitrage[9] model to determine whether securities are correctly priced.

The key idea behind APT model lies on the fact that, in a market in equilibrium, no arbitrage opportunities would exist. Imposing no-arbitrage conditions, Ross ended up with an APT fundamental equation (as SML in CAPM). Noticeably, it could be demonstrated SML equation would be a particular case of APT fundamental equation when only the sensitivity to a single factor (the return on the market portfolio) is considered[10].

---

[8] Ross (1976).

[9] Recall arbitrage definition in section 5.1.

[10] Any interested readers on further information about APT we encourage them to have a look at Blake (2000).

Chapter 9

STOCK ANALYSIS

Recall what we said about the efficient market hypothesis (EMH):

> Market efficiency implies present and future stock prices do not depend on past data, so market prices move randomly and investors cannot predict future movements based on historical series (...). Fama (1965, 1970) divided the EMH into three categories: the weak-form, the semistrong-form and the strong-form of EMH. Under the weak-form EMH, current stock prices fully reflect all currently available market information. Hence, past price, volume and any other historical information would have no relationship with the future direction of security prices, so technical analysis is helpless. Under the assumption of semistrong-form EMH, current stock prices rapidly adjust to the release of any market and non-market information available to the agents. In this case, investors cannot achieve excess returns using fundamental analysis. Finally, the strong-form EMH version implies that prices fully reflect all public and private information. The strong-form EMH assumes perfect markets where information is cost-free and available to all market participants at the same time (...). One essential question arises: which forces guide financial markets behaviour?[1]

Financial industry has always defended—mostly the last twenty years—the tenets of market efficiency in order to justify a model where they have been loosely regulated. It is quite surprising, therefore, that much of the financial industry business is based on the failure of the EMH, either in its semistrong form or even in its weaker form. Because that is indeed what we are assuming when we think we can predict future movements on stock prices based either on their past movements, or based on public company economic data. We are assuming markets are not efficient, so they do not move randomly and asset prices do not fully reflect all public and private information available at any time.

Stock markets provide the opportunity to earn significant profits to anyone able to predict future security price movements. That is the reason why, no matter risks or financial crises, people are increasingly interested in investing on them. They will be also willing to pay for advising, and that is also the reason for so many firms involved or related to the financial industry (asset managers, analysts, traders, magazine experts, professors, journalists, etc.) to be interested in providing such advise. Hundreds of techniques have been claimed to be the ultimate foolproof way to predict market movements, but readers of this book should be aware that these techniques are useful only as a guidance to the investor, because there is no

[1] See chapter 6.

infallible theory that provides the information needed to forecast future at no risk. And there will never be!

Methods for stock analysis could be classified in two groups: technical analysis and fundamental analysis. Both are examined in the next two sections of this chapter. A third category, the so-called behavioural finance, will be examined in chapter 10, providing an insight of forces behind market movements, although it is not yet as developed as technical analysis or fundamental analysis in order to provide rules of thumb to investors.

9.1. Technical Analysis

At the end of nineteenth century, Charles Dow wrote a series of editorials at the Wall Street Journal—the financial newspaper he launched in 1889—where he set the basics of technical analysis. This method based its conclusions exclusively on the analysis of historical prices of securities, and though there is little research that supports Dow Theory, it is still used today by both people on the industry and amateur investors.

Dow theory basically asserts that markets follow several major and minor trends—which could be either bullish or bearish—that are confirmed by volume. That is, when a market moves in a specific direction featuring higher trading volumes, we can assert market participants are anticipating a movement in such direction, so a trend is developing. In 1938, Ralph Elliott published *The Wave Principle*, a book where he tried to apply techniques to forecast those trends, based on the believe that investors move naturally from optimism to pessimism and back again, which develops those trends and waves Dow had anticipated.

Both Dow and Elliott techniques, that laid the basics of technical analysis, are based on crowd psychology. Technical analysis works with two instruments: graphics on one hand, and indicators and oscillators on the other. Dow and Elliott set the basis of chartism (providing buy and sell signals from the analysis of graphics), whereas indicators and oscillators are mathematical equations and ratios developed later, on the sixties and seventies of past century. Some people distinguish two types of analysis here (chartism and technical analysis itself), but most consider them as complementary of the same theory.

Chartism

Technical analysts try to derive trends from market movements. For such purpose, prices are represented in graphs where time is on the x axis and quotations on y axis. They could be plotted in several forms. First, by using line charts that connect close prices with line segments. Second, by means of bar charts, where high and low prices of a trading period determine the length of the bar, and open and close prices are marked with small horizontal lines to the left and the right of the bar, respectively. And third, through candlestick charts, which provide in a single graph more complete information: for every session it shows open and close prices, maximum and minimum prices of the day, and the difference between open and close prices are drown in different colours (called the 'body' of the candlestick, usually coloured in black and white) for uptrend and downtrend movements, respectively.

Following Dow theory, most of those graphs are usually represented with trading volume drawn below. Through them, technical analysts try to determine several patterns for stock market trends. The most common figures they look for are trend lines, lines of support and resistance, changing trends and figures. Trend lines represent the direction the market is following over a specific period of time (which may vary from more than a year for the main trend, to only a few hours for trading purposes). They may be either resistance trend lines or support trend lines, and the combination of both of them determines three basic types of markets: bullish markets (moving up), bearish markets (going down) and lateral markets.

Source: <www.nasdaq.com>.

Figure 33. Bar chart and candlestick chart.

A resistance is a price level which acts as a ceiling for a security price, whereas a support acts as a floor, since at such price level a large group of investors considers it attractive to enter in the market. This way, as the price falls down buying pressure begins to exceed sales, whereas the opposite reasoning works for resistances. Analysts' main objective is to figure out when a market is providing signals of a change in trend to come. That requires a 'breakout', a figure where either a support or a resistance are effectively broken. One method they use for that purpose is to try to identify figures, i.e. classical patterns prices follow from time to time that are classified in two types: reversal patterns and continuation patterns. Some reversal patterns are head and shoulders, hammers, morning stars and shooting stars, whereas continuation patterns are triangles, wedges, flags and tasuki gaps.

Indicators and Oscillators

Indicators are mathematical and statistical calculations from stock price data, usually estimated in order to help chartist analysts in their efforts to determine trends and figures. Likewise a stone thrown into the air slows as it approaches its maximum height, indicators and oscillators warn that if a stock price increases each time at a lower rate (or vice versa), there is probably going to be a reverse in trend.

Basic indicators and oscillators are moving averages, the relative strength index (RSI), stochastic oscillators, MACD oscillator and Fibonacci ratios, among others. Moving averages and exponential moving averages, for example, are useful to remove market noise away. Simple moving averages (SMA) computes the average price of a security over a period of time, whereas exponential moving averages (EMA) reduce the lag by applying more weight to recent prices. On the other hand, we have the RSI, a momentum oscillator that measures the speed at which prices vary, is bounded from 0 to 100, and provides buy and sell signals for level below 30 and above 70 respectively, or the stochastic oscillator, which measures the level of the close prices over a period of time. It has similar boundaries as RSI.

MACD, Moving Average Convergence-Divergence, is also a momentum oscillator that uses two different moving averages (usually 12- and 26-day), subtracting the longer from the shorter, to provide both a trend and a momentum, as follows

$$\text{Standard MACD} = \text{12-day EMA} - \text{26-day EMA}, \tag{34}$$

whereas Fibonacci ratios are used as a guide to determining support lines, resistances and pullbacks (Fibonacci retracements). They are mathematical relationships derived from the Fibonacci numbers (0, 1, 1, 2, 3, 5, 8...).

This has been just a slight overview on technical analysis. Interested readers are encouraged to find more interesting notes on books as Malkiel (2003), also useful for an insight on fundamental analysis we are going to see next.

9.2. Fundamental Analysis

Fundamental analysis supporters claim that though psychology, market noise, trading and speculation have their effect on quotations in short time periods, over the long term market prices adjust to the 'true value' of securities. Such level, called intrinsic value, depends on future expected cash flows of assets, and therefore fundamental analysts base their research on accounting data of companies, financial ratios, expected profits, etc. It performs better than technical analysis under Fama's three categories of EMH, since it fulfils the weak form EMH because fundamental analysis considers that past data is not relevant when predicting the future direction security prices would follow.

When pricing stocks, financial statement analysis becomes essential. The basic instruments fundamental analysts use are valuation methods and financial ratios[2].

Valuation Methods

Through valuation methods analysts try to provide a measure for the intrinsic value of a stock today. Some of the most common techniques are using the expected EPS, the dividend discount model (DDM), the free cash flow (FCF) discount model, the economic value added (EVA) and the market value added (MVA) models.

Expected EPS requires estimating earnings per share, that is, the amount of income a company earns for every share of common stock outstanding, which is the standard for reporting company earnings. When pricing a stock, fundamental analysts try to provide an accurate measure of the expected earnings per share a company is going to earn in the future. This way, if a researcher is able to guess the level of earnings a firm is going to have, she may discount those quantities to the present in order to provide the intrinsic value of such company today. A straight way to calculate expected EPS would be

$$\text{Expected EPS} = \text{Sales per share} \cdot \text{Net profit margin}. \tag{35}$$

Under the DDM—also known as the Gordon-Shapiro model—analysts here try to infer the company's expected future growth and dividend policy[3]. Intrinsic value is then calculated discounting those expected dividends back to their present value. The model ends up with an equation, which simplest expression would be

$$P_0 = \frac{D}{r - g}, \tag{36}$$

where P_0 is the intrinsic value of the share price today, D is the expected dividend, r the required rate of return (the discount rate) and g the expected dividend growth rate in perpetuity. Thus, the price of a stock today depends on future dividends, the company growth rate and the required rate of return (generally interpreted as the rate stockholders require to invest in the company). A nice and simple way to analyze the 'true value' of a company, don't you think?

The FCF model is closely related to the dividend discount model, since it is based on the same procedure, but using FCF[4] instead of dividends as a proper measure to determine the intrinsic value of a company stock. The approach to be used would be as depicted in figure 34. First we define a planning horizon (the next few years, for which we have data enough to

[2] Which both rely on financial statement analysis.

[3] Sometimes expressed as a dividend yield ratio, d, measured as the dividend per share divided by the stock price. It allows to compare the dividend payments by the company to its market capitalization.

[4] The FCF is the money a company makes after it pays for any operational costs and capital expenditures. It measures the income the company makes that is freely available to pay for the capital resources, i.e. the equity and debt. It is defined as Cash flow – Capital expenditures, i.e. as Net income + Depreciation + Change in deferred taxes + Net changes in non-cash current assets and liabilities – Capex.

make predictions), and calculate the free cash flows we expect the company is going to have available to pay for equity and debt. Then, outside the planning horizon, we estimate a constant growth rate in perpetuity we think the company could be able to make on its future cash flows, and calculate the residual value, RV, using the formula

$$RV = FCF_n \cdot \frac{1+g}{r-g}, \tag{37}$$

where FCF_n is the expected free cash flow on the last year of our planning horizon, g is the expected growth rate in perpetuity of the company, and r is the required rate, in this case given by the cost of financing all the company assets, i.e. the WACC[5].

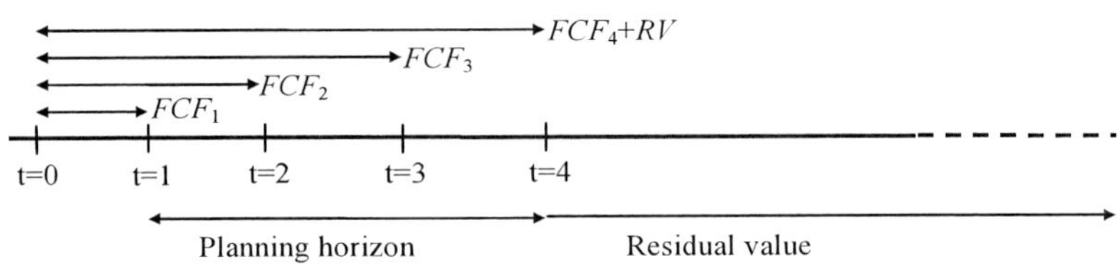

Figure 34. The FCF model.

Finally, we discount those cash flow to present time (t = 0 in figure 34) in order to put them all in ‘present time money’. We shall better see Gordon-Shapiro and FCF models through an example.

Example 15

Sea Corporation, a company financed only with equity, is about to pay to its shareholders in 2011 a dividend of \$1 per share. If we know shareholders of Sea Corp. require a return of 12%, and the company expects to be able to grow at a constant rate in perpetuity of 5%, what is the fundamental value of Sea Corp. shares? Using Gordon-Shapiro DDM (see equation 36), we get P_0 = \$1/(12% – 5%) = \$14,29 per share.

Now we are given the following expected data on Sea Corp. for a planning horizon of four years (data is expressed in million dollars):

	2012	2013	2014	2015
Earnings	60	80	100	100
Cash flows	20	30	38	40
Capital expenditures	10	15	20	20
FCF	10	15	18	20
Taxes	0%	0%	0%	0%
Cost of equity	12%	12%	12%	12%
Cost of debt	8%	8%	8%	8%

[5] WACC stands for weighted average cost of capital. Recall chapter 4.

Beyond 2015 free cash flow is expected to grow in perpetuity at the same rate as the company growth (5%) we detailed before. If the company has 20 million shares outstanding, what is the expected value of a share?[6]

In this case we need to estimate all cash flows (FCFs for the planning horizon are available on data, the residual value must be calculated) and discount them to present using the WACC. Therefore, we first need to calculate the residual value and the WACC. The cost of capital is identical to the cost of equity, that is, 12%. Why? Because we are said the company finances all its assets with equity. If not, we must calculate WACC using equation (11)[7]. Residual value, on the other hand, is calculated through equation (37) as $RV = 20 \cdot (1 + 5\%)/(12\% - 5\%) = 300$.

And now we can discount all future expected cash flows ($10 million in 2012, $15 million in 2013, $18 million in 2014 and $320 million[8] in 2015) at a rate of 12% to get the expected market value of the company. Doing the maths we get a market value of $237.1 million. Since there are 20 million shares outstanding, the fundamental value of Sea Corp shares is $237.1/20 = $11.85 per share.

Regarding EVA and MVA these are measures for relative value analysis, since they provide an estimation of a company value by comparing its ability to add value relative to investment opportunities with a similar level of risk. EVA is an internal measure that uses the profits generated by a company to determine whether it adds value or not. It compares the firm's operating profit (NOPAT) with the opportunity cost of the capital (debt and equity) invested in the company. Formally,

$$\text{EVA} = \text{NOPAT} - \text{WACC} \cdot \text{Capital EVA} \tag{38}$$

and if EVA is positive, the company has earned more than the opportunity cost of capital, so the firm has added value; the contrary holds when EVA is negative. MVA, on the other hand, is a measure of external performance. It accounts for the net present value of all future EVAs by comparing the market value of the company with the amount of capital invested. Formally,

$$\text{MVA} = \text{Market value of the company} - \text{Capital}, \tag{39}$$

and performance is measured by changes in MVA through time[9].

Financial Ratios

Financial ratios, on the other hand, allow for comparison between peer companies[10]. Four commonly used are price to earnings ratio, return on equity, price to book ratio, and price to cash flow ratio. The price to earnings ratio (PER) is defined as

---

[6] Recall we said Sea Corp. finances only with equity.
[7] See chapter 4.
[8] Remember the residual value at 2015 must also be discounted.
[9] EVA® and MVA are intellectual property of Stern Stewart & Co. See <www.sternstewart.com>.
[10] Peer companies are firms operating in the same sector.

$$\text{PER} = \frac{\text{Price}}{\text{Earnings per share}}, \tag{40}$$

and is a measure of how profitable a company is. What PER compares is how many times profits are included on the stock price, so it gives a nice straight measure whether a security is expensive or cheap on the market when compared to peers or historically against its own past data. On the other hand, return on equity (ROE) is given by

$$\text{ROE} = \frac{\text{Net income}}{\text{Equity}}, \tag{41}$$

and represents the rate of return the company generates per dollar invested. Likewise, the return on total assets (ROA) is

$$\text{ROA} = \frac{\text{Net income}}{\text{Total assets}}. \tag{42}$$

Both ROE and ROA are the most commonly used ratios to measure the profitability of a company. The highest those two ratios, the better. In turn, the price to book ratio (P/B) is

$$\text{P/B} = \frac{\text{Price}}{\text{Book value}}, \tag{43}$$

where book value is the value of the company according to its balance sheet. It can be rearranged as

$$\text{P/B} = \text{PER} \cdot \text{ROE} \tag{44}$$

using PER and ROE defined in equations (40) and (41) above. Finally, price to cash flow ratio (P/CF) compares the company value to the cash flows generated, as follows

$$\text{P/CF} = (\text{Company value}) / (\text{Cash flow}). \tag{45}$$

Analysts would use those ratios above to compare the performance of companies of different size and across economic sectors. Again, we suggest interested readers to have a deeper insight on valuation methods—and fundamental analysis generally speaking—in books like Brealey and Myers (2003). But before proceeding with the section on behavioural finance, we wish to end our insight on technical and fundamental analysis with a classical innuendo...

Asset Management Industry

Banking industry claims the least regulated financial markets are, the most efficient they will be, but at the same time they claim for efficiency, a large stake of their revenues come from the asset management industry. Most financial institutions own asset management firms through which they provide customers with services such as market analysis, portfolio management, security recommendation, etc., but we should not forget the EMH implies present and future stock prices do not depend on past data, so market prices move randomly and investors cannot predict future movements.

One of the two could be true—either markets are efficient or asset management industry is able to over-perform—but not both. If you claim markets are efficient, then no asset manager would be able to consistently outperform the market, no matter which techniques they use. And on the contrary, if asset management firms sale their services claiming to be able to outperform, what they are saying is that markets do not meet the EMH. What a contradiction, isn't it?

Asset management industry uses all theoretical models we have seen before (Markowitz portfolio theory, asset pricing models, technical analysis, fundamental analysis, etc.) in order to determine which assets are underpriced on the market, and provides its customers diversified portfolios to maximize their expected return over their life investment horizon, while minimizing risks assumed.

Some common approaches used to provide market recommendations are top-down vs. bottom-up, value vs. growth, and active vs. passive management. The top-down analysis is a three step approach that starts with a forecast of future economic data for the whole economy. Based on this study, they project that data over industries in the economy, in order to determine different predictions for each of them. Finally, they select the securities expected to outperform based on those economic and industry forecasts. On bottom-up analysis—also called 'stock picking' approach—the asset manager simply picks underpriced stocks, regardless the economic situation or industry trends.

Value investing looks for stocks on the market that are underpriced, that is, that their intrinsic value is well below their observed price on the market. On the contrary, growth stocks may be overpriced today in terms of PER and other ratios, but they would be bought by growth investors under the expectation that those companies will exhibit above-average growth in the future. Most studies claim value outperforms growth, though for some periods (for example, during the dot-com bubble) growth outperformed. Therefore, most analysts consider a truly diversified portfolio should have both value and growth stocks.

Finally, benchmarking is a more consistent strategy with the EMH. If markets are efficient and therefore investors cannot predict future price movements to consistently outperform the market, what rational investors should do is to peg their investments to a market index. Obviously, this kind of investment is less attractive to the asset management industry due to its lower management fees and, therefore, its lower profitability. Hence, we should differentiate active management, where asset managers try to outperform the market, from passive management, where managers try just to replicate the index.

Chapter 10

BEHAVIOURAL FINANCE

Traditional finance assumes investors take rational decisions. Besides, since they are all rational and risk averse, they always try to diversify their investments through a portfolio perspective. In 1979 Daniel Kahneman and Amos Tversky presented their *critique of expected utility theory as a descriptive model of decision making under risk, developing an alternative model, called prospect theory*[1]. There they claimed people, when taking financial decisions under a context of uncertainty, exhibit deviations from rationality not previously considered. To illustrate, perhaps the two most relevant deviations suggested by Kahneman and Tversky (1979) are the certainty effect and the isolation effect. By the certainty effect individuals underweight outcomes that are merely probable in comparison with outcomes that are obtained with certainty. The isolation effect in turn is responsible of inconsistent preferences when the same choice is presented in different forms.

Psychological attributes of investors under BF

- Loss aversion
- Biased expectations
- Asset segmentation

The consideration of these effects raises a new paradigm. They laid the foundation of behavioural finance, a discipline that considers investors exhibit three basic psychological characteristics different from those assumed by traditional finance: loss aversion, biased expectations and asset segmentation. Under this approach, for example, investors would not be risk averse, but exhibit loss aversion (that is, they prefer larger uncertain losses to smaller certain losses). As a consequence, people act as 'addicted gamblers' preferring not to give up when they face a small loss, keeping their investments on, and taking their chances on a larger loss while there is still a possibility to recover their money. The biased expectations suggest that, instead of a world where investors use all relevant information on the market to set their forecasts, they overestimate their abilities. Investors believe that their expectations are more likely to be realized, so they discard information that does not support their choices. Overconfidence could be a good explanation for such behaviour. Finally, due to asset segmentation, investors would focus their attention only on individual asset's risk-return characteristics, so they do not evaluate a particular investment's impact on the overall portfolio position, as portfolio theory says.

[1] Kahneman and Tversky (1979), p. 263.

Behavioural finance asserts, therefore, that the asset valuation process incorporates not only economic variables, but psychological variables too. That is the reason why technical analysts consider behavioural finance could also be interpreted as a background rationale for technical analysis. If we want to analyze the economic decisions of agents in the market (not only of 'naive investors', but of analysts, traders, institutions and 'experts' too), we must pay attention to cognitive biases and emotional factors that affect consumers, borrowers and investors decision-making processes.

10.1. THE PSYCHOLOGY OF INVESTING

Behavioural finance studies how people's 'psychological anchors' often cause investors to behave irrationally, make systematic mistakes that violate standard finance assumptions, or base their investment decisions on emotions like greed, fear and herd instinct.

Shefrin's (2002)[2] argument that a few psychological phenomena pervade the entire landscape of finance led him to distinguish two main sources of psychological biases: heuristics and framing biases. Heuristics are concerned with the way people select relevant information from all data available. They express the idea that people make decisions based on 'rules of thumb', not necessarily logic. Framing biases, on the other hand, suggest that how a problem is presented—and not the data set itself—could determine market participants' behaviour and their choices. The idea behind these psychological terms is that people need to filter information through proxies, since market data is vast and changes every second, and that filtering process may be affected by cognitive or emotional biases.

Heuristics biases

- Overconfidence
- Availability
- Anchoring and conservatism
- Representativeness
- Familiarity and home bias

Some heuristics investors exhibit are, to illustrate, overconfidence and availability heuristic. Due to overconfidence, many people would tend to think that either the information they handle is better than average, or they are better able to interpret it. Availability heuristic, on the other hand, would be the tendency to pay attention to pieces of information that are easier to get or understand. Anchoring (being influenced by irrelevant or non informative data) and conservatism (the tendency to under-

[2] For further info, see Shleifer (2000), Shefrin (2002), and Hens and Bachmann (2008).

react to news) are two related concepts often mentioned on behavioural finance empirical research.

Other investors tend to view a 'good company' as a 'good stock', when in fact the same security could be either a good or a bad stock at two different points in time, depending whether they are underpriced or not. Those investors would probably exhibit representativeness, that is, a reliance on stereotypes that could also lead to gambler's fallacy (identifying patterns in truly random sequences). Finally, familiarity and aversion to ambiguity would explain why people use to buy stocks of companies they are familiar with. Doing so, they underweight international market stocks—what is also known as a home bias—and the resulting portfolio would be poorly diversified.

On the other hand, framing biases are, for example, those two on which Kahneman and Tversky (1979) based their prospect theory, that is, mental accounting and loss aversion. Mental accounting is the tendency to look at individual stocks rather than the overall portfolio performance, contradicting Modern Portfolio Theory, whereas loss aversion is the preference for larger uncertain losses to smaller certain losses.

Framing biases

- Loss aversion
- Mental accounting
  - Money illusion effect
  - House money effect
  - Disposition effect
  - Endowment effect

Four concepts related to mental accounting that are commonly exhibited by investors are money illusion effect, house money effect, disposition effect and endowment effect. Money illusion—a term coined by John M. Keynes—refers to the fact that many consumers and investors think of currency in nominal rather than real terms. We could see it clearly during 2009-2010, when people thought of deposits in the Eurozone at 1% as unfair (when the inflation in most European markets was about zero), whereas years before they felt being well-paid with deposits at 4% when inflation in some European countries like Spain, for example, was well above 5% (so they actually were facing a negative real return). House money effect expresses the idea that, after winning some money on the markets, many investors tend to treat their gains as house money, i.e. money that is not of their own, investing them in riskier assets. Under disposition effect investors hold losers too long and sell winners too early, whereas the endowment effect predicts people will keep their existing portfolio unchanged, no matter the expected risk and return characteristics of the assets on the market. This is very common when people are linked to a particular asset for sentimental reasons (family heritage...).

Other effects

- Reference points
- Try-to-break-even effect
- Long-shot bias
- Chasing performance
- Preference for dividends

And we can still find more biases. Many people, for example, use reference points to take buy and sell decisions (not to sell a stock until its price reaches the maximum level on record, for example). Similarly, investors exhibiting the trying-to-break-even effect will be willing to take high risk investments to recover from losses experienced before. Some other plausible explanations for other common agent's behaviour on the stock markets would be the long-shot bias (a gambling tendency to bet on highly unlikely events), chasing performance (another common mistake where investors like to purchase past winners, which evidence shows tend to under-perform in the future) or the investor's preference for dividends, a quite common empirical evidence that contradicts the

Modigliani-Miller dividend irrelevance theorem. The explanation for this behaviour would be that investors use a sort of combination of loss aversion and mental accounting so they separate their investments into a capital gains account and a dividend account. Cutting the dividend here would be interpreted as a loss in the dividend account, so investors would be reluctant to do so.

Shefrin (2002) proposed that all of us exhibit those biases above because our rational thinking is influenced by cognitive and emotional biases. People for example exhibit cognitive framing and cognitive dissonance. The former refers to a collection of anecdotes and stereotypes people experiment through their lifetimes. Then, the choices they make are influenced by those emotional filters. Tversky and Kahneman (1979) showed that the way a problem is presented can affect the outcome in a way that rationality does not hold, which led to the development of prospect theory, as explained above. And a person can experiment cognitive dissonance when her actions differ from her personal beliefs. In order to avoid cognitive dissonance when investing, we tend to underestimate past mistakes overestimating successes.

Emotional biases, on the other hand, would be for example greed, fear and herd instinct, which are said to be the three basic emotional motivators of stock markets' volatility. Fear of regret leads investors to hold assets for too long when they made a bad investment. Seeking of pride, on the contrary, leads them to sell too quickly when they have a profitable investment just to feel proud of their success. In turn, the snake-bite effect—somewhat the contrary of the try-to-break-even effect—stands for the unwillingness to take more risks after experiencing losses. Investors will avoid riskier stocks after they have been bitten by the snake of a loss in the stock market!

Readers may agree that, even though we could go further in this analysis, all these suggestions allow us to conclude it seems reasonable to wonder whether investors in capital markets do indeed behave rationally at any time.

10.2. ... And More

Through history, financial markets have also experienced some events that cannot be explained under a rational investor approach. Some are related to behavioural finance concepts, as we shall see next. We should name first an event that has been repeating for centuries and which, nonetheless, it is not really a financial event simply because it is a fraud. In any case, we should stop and think for a while why our society seems inclined to fall again and again in these types of deception.

Naturally Occurring Ponzi Processes

Ponzi schemes are a fraudulent pyramidal investment where the profits that early investors receive come actually from the money contributed by new investors. The scheme is named after Carlo Ponzi, an anonymous Italian immigrant in Boston who became millionaire in six months promising investors to 'double their money in 90 days', in year 1920. If we analyze market trends over long periods of time, it seems that natural Ponzi processes—not fraudulent this time—appear as well from time to time. The recent great bull market we are going to see next could be mentioned as one of them, but the first documented naturally occurring Ponzi scheme was the *Tulipmania*, back in Netherlands in the first half of the 17th century.

The Great Bull Market

Dow Jones Industrial Average index needed more than 60 years to multiply its value ten times (from 100 to 1,000 points between 1920 and 1983), but it only took 15 years to repeat that once again (from 1,000 to 10,000 points between 1983 and 1999). At that point, several companies quoting at that index had PER ratios well above 100 (long term ratios on the US stock markets have averaged 20). The reason behind such market behaviour was that people truly believed we were entering in a new era. Some historical facts seemed to confirm that: the fall of communism, the appearance of new technologies (internet, mobile phones), the globalization, low inflation, etc. All of that made people more confident on our economic system and the risk aversion level of the society as a whole fall dramatically. But in fact, if inflation was low, expected returns for both risky and riskless investments should be lower as well. On the contrary, the fall on risk aversion and the fact that new people was entering the market—many of them probably investing in stocks for the first time in their lives—made markets soar. Time put things in place, as we would see during the first decade of the 21st century.

The Age Wave

The age wave is a demographic phenomenon that could affect long-term market performance. From time to time a generation with birth rates much higher than the previous and following generations appears. It is what they call a baby boom. When years after those baby boomers retire, it could happen that when they try to cash the wealth they have been accumulating at record levels, the generation coming have not enough money to buy those assets, so asset prices fall. It is said that Western economies have not faced that problem so far because though they have not grown fast enough to absorb the baby boomers assets, emerging economies did. As China, India, Brazil and some other countries in Asia and Africa emerge and become wealthier, they would be purchasing the excess assets of the developed world.

Optimistic Forecasts

Some researchers have warned that the financial industry tends to release optimistic forecasts and recommendations, and therefore promoting investors overconfidence. Some reasons behind such behaviour are that many analysts work for companies that also provide investment banking services, the lack of sell recommendations (attributed to the analyst's fear of losing access to company information), or the influence of their colleagues, because it is safer for an analyst to follow the overall trend than going against it.

PART III: THE FINANCIAL MELTDOWN AND THE GREAT RECESSION (AFTER THE GREAT MODERATION)

Perhaps readers would agree that a book about financial markets written these days should not left out the details concerning the origins of the Great Recession that began on August 2007 and affected Western economies mainly. To fulfil that goal, we devote the last part of the book to offer our view on the causes and consequences of the financial meltdown and the Great Recession that followed.

Starting from the years of the so-called 'Great Moderation', when risk aversion in our societies fell to the minimum level, the main goal of this part is twofold. First, to analyse the basic 'antecedents' that led to the financial meltdown: namely, the credit expansion and the housing boom in most Western economies, the speculative use of derivatives on a massive scale, a long period of—probably not justified—low interest rates, especially in the U.S. economy, and the substantial global imbalances generated during the last two decades of globalization. Second, to offer a step-by-step explanation on how the financial meltdown occurred, as well as the consequences of the Great Depression that followed.

To this end, the layout of this part of the book is as follows. Chapter 11 provides a brief intro suggesting that the roots of the present crisis come from at least two decades ago. In chapter 12 we describe the four basic antecedents that led to the crisis. In chapter 13 a description of the 2007-2008 financial meltdown is done. Finally, in chapter 14 we analyze the subsequent Great Recession we are still suffering today.

Chapter 11

SPECULATIVE VOLATILITY IN A FREE SOCIETY[1]

"Since becoming a central banker, I have learned to mumble with great incoherence. If I turn out to be particularly clear you've probably misunderstood what I've said"
Speaking to a Senate Committee in 1987 - Alan Greenspan

When did the present crisis begin? It is generally accepted that 'subprime' mortgages triggered the financial meltdown, but really the origins must be set much further back. We might use as a symbol the key date of November 9th, 1989. That day not only the Berlin Wall fell down, but a new era began: capitalism had triumphed over communism, and the more than forty years of ideological confrontation came to an end. Right after that, the last decade of the 20th century saw the emergence of a new economic and political worldwide scenario: the 'globalization'. Internet and mobile phones could be considered its most prominent sign of identity among common people (it is amazing to realize now that in 1989 most of us had never heard about Internet and mobile phones, right?), but it really encompasses much more: protectionism[2] was reduced while international trade developed exponentially; the Euro currency was born as the ultimate step of the E.U. economic integration; and finally, the most important 'globalization' of them all, the capital markets integration worldwide.

A new paradigm dominated the political scenario since then: giving all power to the governments (communism) had lost the battle against giving all power to the markets (liberal capitalism). Hence, the more market liberalization and the smaller the role of the State in the economy, the better. Neo-liberal economic ideas prevailed since then for over two decades.

From mid nineties, stock markets started to boost. Dow Jones Industrial Average Index (DJIA) depicted in figure 35 may be used to see it clearly.

---

[1] A must-read recommendation here is Robert Shiller's (2000) *Irrational Exuberance*, a classic book where Professor Shiller anticipated the dot-com bubble collapse based on research in areas as diverse as psychology, sociology, media or demography. Some of his thoughts are also implicit in this essay about the present crisis, since we feel both episodes are related somehow.

[2] As opposed to free trade, protectionism is an economic policy that seeks to protect a domestic economy from a competitive environment by imposing restrictions to trade, such as tariffs (a tax on imported goods) quotas (limits on the quantity of a good to be traded) or restrictive regulation.

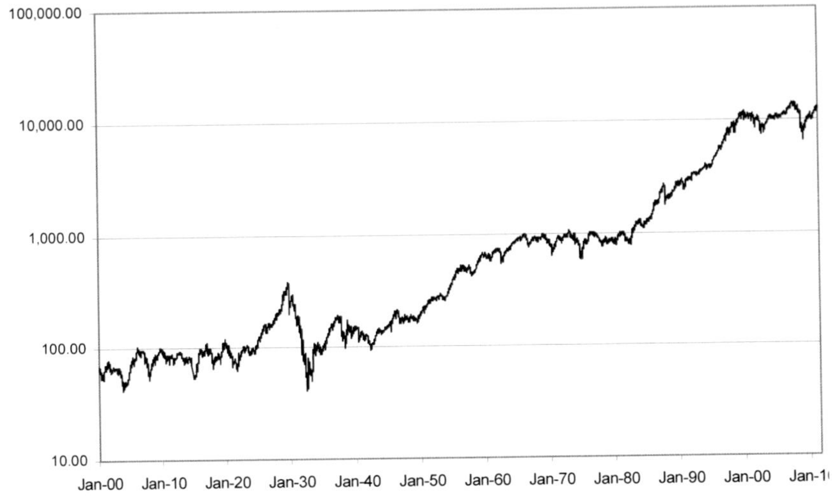

Figure 35. Dow Jones Industrial Average Index (DJIA).

DJIA index needed more than sixty years to grow ten times its value (from 100 points in 1920 to 1,000 points in 1983), but it just required fifteen years to do that again (rising from 1,000 to 10,000 points between 1983 and 1999). We see two main reasons explaining such performance. First, risk aversion in our societies fell to the minimum level. People's confidence in our economic system soared, leading all kinds of agents—from institutions to many families without any experience in financial markets—to invest their savings in the most speculative securities. Second, the development of new technologies, Internet, the globalization... pointed out the direction our society was addressing the following years. Combining those two facts we ended up experiencing the dot-com bubble in the 1990s, a naturally occurring Ponzi process where new money kept entering the market, attracted by high returns offered, until it all collapsed in year 2000. In fact, those days analysts paid more attention to a new index—the NASDAQ index—rather than the DJIA index. Its graph depicted in figure 36 says it all: it multiplied its value almost twenty times in just eight years. Unbelievable!

In 1978 Charles Kindleberger[3] offered a nice description of how price bubbles developed in different markets through history. They all resemble what we described above. First, they start with some good news: mosaic viruses producing nice looking tulips before the Dutch *Tulipmania* in the 1630s, rapidly growing trade between Europe and the New World before the Mississippi bubble in 1720, new means of transportation during the British first railway boom in 1845, or fast growth and rapid expansion of mass production during the 1920s before the Great Depression. Then, after the good news come, people's confidence pushes things far beyond the limits.

[3] The fifth edition of 'Manias, panics and crashes' (2005) was authored by Charles Kindleberger and Robert Aliber.

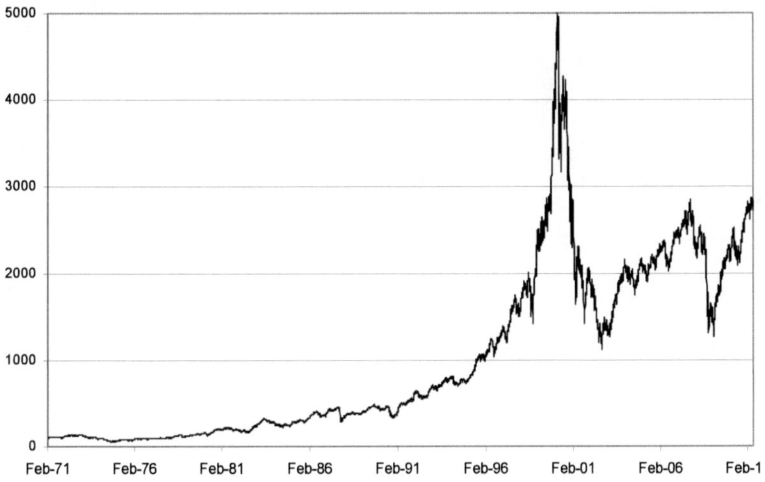

Figure 36. NASDAQ Composite index.

The story repeated once again after their analysis—after all, we are only human—so during the nineties we saw the emergence of the dot-com bubble. But what Kindleberger (1978) also suggested was that, after the initial good news and the rise in confidence, for the bubble to be sustainable it is needed some sort of amplification mechanism. And it is quite remarkable that this role has been played, very often, by credit and derivatives (which are, basically, just another form of credit). After good news appear and markets start offering higher returns, people start expecting this series will be continued on time almost endlessly, so their risk perception diminishes and they start to live on credit. To illustrate, the first time a futures market was developed in Europe was, indeed, during the *Tulipmania*, and all price bubbles through history have witnessed the highest records of credit and speculation. Think of the days before the 1929 crash, for example. Or not so long ago, think of our economic crisis today, too.

Chapter 12

THE ANTECEDENTS

Several factors—not just one, we are indeed analyzing a much more complex situation than that—could be mentioned that bred this worldwide crisis: the credit expansion and the housing boom in most Western economies, the speculative use of derivatives on a massive scale, a long period of—probably not justified—low interest rates, especially in the U.S., or the substantial global imbalances generated during the last two decades of globalization are among them. Why economists did not realize so many threats jeopardizing the world's economy? Well, first of all, it is not true that economists did not realize the existence of those potential instabilities: in fact there is plenty of academic literature and even warnings from monetary and government authorities about the potential dangers of excessive indebtedness, the housing bubble and others. But it is indeed true that what no one seemed to foresee was that the combination of all those factors could lead to a sort of 'perfect storm' in which we are involved now. Perhaps we should interpret this as a warning about the necessity of a greater degree of relation within economics and between economics and other social sciences, as well as the need of a world authority that patrols the economic performance in a globally integrated economy as we have now.

12.1. CREDIT EXPANSION AND HOUSING BOOM

In short, overconfidence led most economic agents believe that good times would last forever. We had entered into a 'one-world vision' with no ideological dispute, where we were able to perform a long-period of sustainable economic growth and controlled low inflation, where relevant emerging economies as China, India or Brazil rapidly developed and became integrated in the global market economy, and where technological advances such as internet or mobile phones heralded *this time is different*[1].

The money that ran out of the stock markets during the dot-com bubble crash sought refuge in the real estate market. It is amazing to see how multiple housing booms developed simultaneously during the same period of time in distant countries as the U.S., Ireland, Spain, Russia, Singapore, China or the Arab Emirates. The raise of real estate prices had also a

[1] 'This time is different' is the title of a well-known and highly recommendable book by Carmen Reinhart and Kenneth Rogoff. See Reinhart and Rogoff (2009).

wealth effect that reinforced people's perception on the economic situation, so a combination of a lower risk aversion and overconfident expectations increased the demand for credit, which in turn provided more feedback to the housing bubble that was developing. Charles Bean[2] provides the increase on the ratio of household and business financial liabilities to GDP between 1995 and 2007 as a measure of the credit boom dimension in countries like the U.K. (rose from 128 to 213% within that period) or Spain (from 77 to 214%). It is worth mention that the other antecedents we will see next—especially the loose monetary policies and the global imbalances—also helped feeding this extraordinary credit expansion. But these data could be also used to interpret the Great Recession in an alternative manner: during the credit boom we have lived 'several years in advance', ahead of our possibilities, so this crisis would be simply a period needed to step back to a more sustainable growth path.

Finally, the credit and housing booms have also revealed a financial sector unable to make a proper evaluation of credit demand and the risks involved, and where incentives might have proved ineffective to avoid misconduct within the industry. In fact, it is not just a matter of banks not being able to detect when they are understating risks, it is a matter that maybe they are aware of them, but not following the trend would leave them 'out of the game' (whereas) following competitors' behaviour reduces risk of underperformance[3].

12.2. Derivatives: Hedging vs. Speculation

As we have seen in section 5.2 the primary function of derivatives—the reason why they were originally developed in the Chicago Board of Trade during the mid 19th century—was hedging, i.e. to provide insurance against many type of risks investors face. Since their payoffs depend on another financial instrument or asset, they allow risks on the underlying asset to be transferred from one party to another.

But if hedging were the only aim for using derivatives, it would not make sense the market volume that is negotiated yearly on those markets. Let us recall here[4] figure 15, where we saw that, during the last years—even after the credit crunch—on derivatives market the volume negotiated accounted for a total amount outstanding of more than ten times the world's GDP. Do we need insurance every year for a value more than ten times the total output produced by our economies during that period? It does not seem reasonable.

This extraordinary development of derivatives markets has taken place mostly during the first decade of 21st century, and it was based mainly on speculation. Derivatives markets are more liquid, have lower capital requirements—allowing engaging in leveraged positions—and offer lower transaction costs than securities markets. This makes derivatives usually more attractive to invest, especially for speculative purposes (trying to profit from betting on the future value of the underlying asset). Since they allow to engage in leveraged positions, they make it easier to earn large returns (or losses!) with small movements in the underlying asset's price, so speculators—who seek maximizing profits on their investments in the shortest period of time and providing the minimum possible funds of their own—widely use them.

---

[2] Bean (2010).

[3] See Peón and Calvo (2010).

[4] See the derivatives section in part I.

The use of derivatives had a relevant influence on the 2007-2008 financial meltdown. Their use through the development of instruments such as collateralized debt obligations (CDOs) or credit default swaps (CDS)[5] increased the risk appetite of investors and reduced the risk perception of financial institutions and supervisors. It could be interpreted as hedging the first issuances of those instruments by banks willing to securitize mortgages on their balance sheet, but that was rapidly followed by a speculative 'search for yield'[6] of investors and a 'regulation arbitrage' by financial institutions which, given the legal permission that allowed them to leave these derivative instruments off-balance sheet, tried to take advantage by increasing those practices to the maximum without being required to increase capital.

What defenders of unregulated derivatives markets claim (Fed's former Chairman, Alan Greenspan, was the most representative among them, and now even he has acknowledged his *shocked disbelief*[7]) is that derivatives are not the problem, but the use investors made of them. As a comparison, it would be the same as selling fire insurance contracts to arsonists. Against them are those who believe that precisely the main weakness of unregulated derivatives markets is that they have been proved to be exposed to fraudulent practices, or morally dubious at least.

12.3. Monetary Policies

In the U.S. the Federal Reserve monetary policy from 2002 to 2006 has been criticized for being too loose. After the dot-com crash, fears that the American economy could be falling into a Japan-style 'lost decade' induced American authorities to promote a 'cheap money' policy during a long period of time as the best way to avoid that possibility. Interest rates were between 2 and 4 percent points below the appropriate policy suggested by the Taylor rule[8] during almost 4 years, which could have boosted the credit bubble.

12.4. Global Imbalances

The years before the financial meltdown have witnessed the highest current account imbalances across countries ever. More interestingly, those imbalances are counterintuitive to those one would expect. In Bean's words,

The rapid development and integration into the global market economy of China, India, Brazil and other emerging market economies might have been expected to lead to capital

5 Recall CDS's description in the derivatives section, and CDOs in the debt markets section, both in part I.

6 The low level of real returns on bonds during periods when central banks promote a low-interest-rates monetary policy encourage investors and financial institutions to shift into riskier assets that offer higher returns. That behaviour is known as a 'search for yield'.

7 *Self-regulation by Wall Street had failed. Those of us who have looked to the self-interest of lending institutions to protect shareholder's equity–myself especially–are in a state of shocked disbelief.* (Alan Greenspan, testifying before the U.S. Congress on October 23rd, 2008.) Source: <www.independent.co.uk>.

8 The Taylor rule (Taylor, 1993) suggests a level of suitable interest rates for an economy based on its inflation and GDP performance, and is commonly used by central banks as a guideline for their monetary policies. It is given by the formula $i=\pi+r^*+a\cdot(\pi-\pi^*)+b\cdot(y-y^*)$, where i stands for interest rate, π and π^* are the actual rate of inflation (measured by the GDP deflator) and the desired rate of inflation, respectively, y and y^* are the logarithm of the real GDP output and of the potential GDP output, respectively, r^* is the equilibrium real interest rate that wants to be set, and a and b are parameters.

flows from the advanced countries into these economies in order to provide the investment to equip the extra workers being brought on the global labour market. Instead, we saw China and some other emerging market economies running large current account surpluses and exporting capital, whereas countries such as the U.S. and the U.K. ran current account deficits and imported capital[9].

Countries like Ireland, the U.K., Spain or the U.S. run their highest current account deficits ever—which could even reach figures of 10% of GDP—financed by countries like Norway, Germany, Russia, most OPEC countries and, namely, China, which ran figures of current account surplus above 11% of its GDP by 2007.

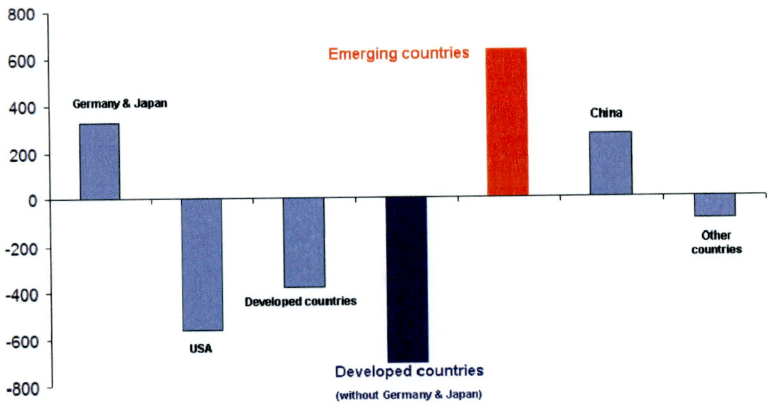

Source: CIA World Factbook.

Figure 37. Current account balances: Emerging vs. developed economies (in billions of U.S. dollars).

Those trade deficits and surplus generated capital flows that probably fostered credit growth and fed housing bubbles all over the world as we mentioned earlier. Not surprisingly, countries with worse current account balances like U.S., Spain, Ireland, U.K., and others, are among those who are suffering the most the consequences of the Great Recession while the main creditors are among those who have already emerged from it or are starting to do it more easily than the former (China and other emerging countries, Netherlands and Germany compared to other E.U. members).

---

[9] Bean (2010), p. 299.

Chapter 13

THE 2007-2008 FINANCIAL MELTDOWN

As we saw in part I, financial markets are fiduciary, that is, they are based on faith about the good functioning of our economic system. Recalling our words,

> (...) keep in mind this fiduciary nature of financial markets, because this fact explains both the extraordinary development they have achieved in Western capitalist economies, as well as their inherent instability[1].

Any event that makes people 'lose their faith' in the good functioning of the markets could potentially cause severe damage to the economy, and this is indeed what happened during the financial meltdown, as we are going to describe next.

Subprime mortgages were the fuse that ignited the credit crisis and caused the worldwide financial panic, but readers should be aware that 'bank runs' actually occur quite frequently and usually for the same reason: a liquidity crisis. The process that started on August 2007 with the first liquidity problems on the mortgage-backed securities markets developed into another 'bank run', but this time to a global scale, a so-called 'wholesale run' so severe that could only be compared with the collapse of the global banking system during the Great Depression.

As we saw in the previous section, the origins of the present crisis were the credit and housing booms almost everywhere together with the wide increase in the use of derivatives for speculative purposes that allowed financial institutions to sell those mortgage risks through securitization to investors willing to engage riskier investments in order to achieve higher returns. With the raise of interest rates during 2006 and 2007, the chain reaction began: the first home buyers in the U.S. market could not pay their mortgages and on the real estate market prices started to unexpectedly fall sharply. This had a double effect on securitization vehicles like CDOs: on one hand they started losing value because they depended on people paying their mortgages, and on the other hand the collateral behind those derivatives—the property value—was also diminishing.

Losses on subprime mortgage securities were just the beginning of the process. If those would had been the only damages to financial institutions, then probably most banks, which had recently gone through several years of high-profit generation, could had been able to bear the situation with not much problem. The Fed estimated in 2007 the expected losses on the

---

[1] See section 1.2.

subprime mortgage market to sum up about $50 billion in the U.S., whereas two years later the IMF provided a figure of no less than $3.4 trillion[2]. Why that difference? What happened is that the subprime crisis triggered a liquidity crisis that blew out confidence on financial markets[3].

Our key word from now on will be liquidity. Contrary to what many people identify as similar concepts, money and liquidity are not the same thing. Money is indeed the most liquid asset by definition[4] so that is the reason why many people think of money when we talk about liquidity. Liquidity is actually the probability that an asset can be converted to an expected value within a specific period of time and without causing a significant change in its price. A bank—any business generally speaking—might face a liquidity problem although being a perfectly profitable company. That is why one of the basic tasks of any company's financial department is to manage the timing of their 'cash flows', because any mismatch leaving the cash account with not funds enough to face a required payment would make the company either to sell assets urgently—probably with a significant drop in its price—or to negotiate with its creditors the deferral of payments coming—probably at worse conditions.

This liquidity problem was progressively worsening. Any fixed income security that was suspected to be backed by a subprime mortgage begun to lose value aggressively (with BBB tranches[5] losing up to 20% of their value within a few days). Financial institutions facing a liquidity problem found out then that when trying to sell a CDO rated BBB, they were paid about 60% of their value a few months ago. This situation generated an adverse selection dilemma: if a bank was willing to sell an asset, the counterparty would interpret this as the financial institution trying to get rid of a 'lemon'[6]. Apart from the effects on the ABS markets, this liquidity crisis started stressing the interbank money market where banks suspected to be affected could not get financing even paying interest rates well above the official Euribor/Libor rates.

Some other banks that also had subprime securities on their balance sheet might believe they were not affected by these events, because since they were not facing any liquidity problem, they needed not to undersell them. But then they would be wrong: mark-to-market accounting requires any asset on the balance sheet of a company to be valued at its fair value based on the current market price. This forced companies to reflect huge losses on their accounting and provisioning resources enough to cope with them. More banks—now most of them both in the U.S. and Europe—got involved in the liquidity crunch, triggering a devastating crisis of confidence within the banking industry. No bank was willing to lend or was able to borrow any funds from the market, so money markets dried out completely.

---

[2] See Bean (2010).

[3] Goodhart et al. (2010) put that idea this other way: '(...) concerns about liquidity and default interact. (...) the economic shock arising from the U.S. housing market and its effect on MBS raised the prospect of a higher probability of default amongst an increasing range of banks and their associated conduits. This concern (...) led to a reduction in market liquidity and hence to a fall in asset prices (which) reinforced concerns about banks' and other financial intermediaries' solvency, and this further reduced liquidity in a range of asset markets, with a variety of self-amplifying spirals then bringing the whole financial system to its knees'.

[4] Recall what we saw about 'money supply' in section 2.2.

[5] As we described, CDO are divided into tranches, each one receiving a credit rating.

[6] The term 'lemon' was first coined by American economist George Akerlof in his acclaimed work of 1970, where he set the background on asymmetric information and adverse selection analyzing the market for used cars, where bad cars ('lemons') eventually drive out the good ones.

Central Banks immediately began to flood the markets with liquidity in volumes never seen before, while also aggressively cutting their policy rates back (the Fed, for example, reduced the federal fund rate from 4.25 to 2% within the first weeks of 2008[7]). They promoted monetary policy actions day after day, and sometimes through coordinated efforts by Central Banks of the U.S., the Eurozone, the U.K. and Japan, intending to restore confidence by proving they would do 'whatever it might be necessary'. They did: the Fed more than doubled its assets[8], whereas the Bank of England tripled them within the month right after the Lehman Brothers collapse. In figure 38 we may see how the ratio of M3 to the monetary base (MB) in the U.S. fell sharply. As we have seen[9], MB includes all money issued by the Central Bank. The ratio fell to less than a half basically because MB more than doubled due to the liquidity expansion promoted by the FED.

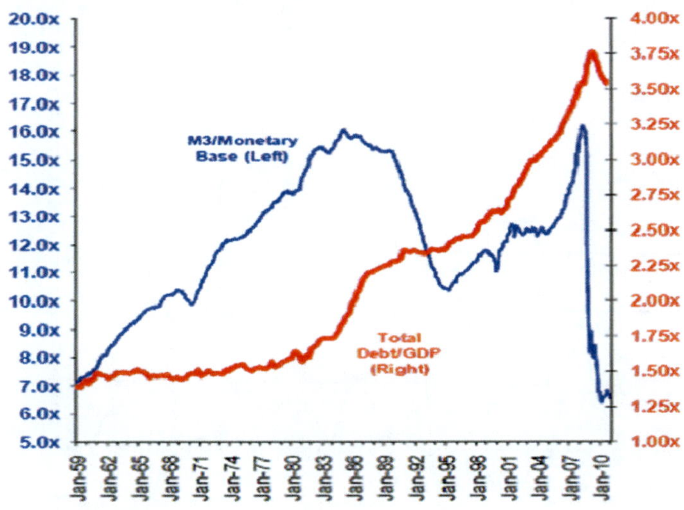

Figure 38. U.S. total (public and private) debt outstanding.

After several names being affected (Nothern Rock, Bear Stearns, Fannie Mae, Freddie Mac...) it was the Lehman Brothers collapse—and Merrill Lynch 'saved by the bell' that same day, September 15th, 2008—what triggered panic. American authorities were not willing to rescue Lehman Brothers in order to give a warning to other financial institutions: *we will not allow those who have behaved wrongly, or had not been prudent assessing risks, to be rescued.* This is in fact what it must be done in order to prevent 'moral hazard'[10] within the banking industry. But just one day later, American International Group (AIG), the largest insurance company worldwide, collapsed in the stock market because it seemed obvious it was not going to be able to meet the increasing collateral obligations on credit default swaps

[7] See figure 3 in chapter 2.

[8] That is indeed what providing liquidity to the market means, not giving banks money out of nothing, but buying the fixed income securities banks are willing to sell on the market but can find no buyer. Recall in part I we explained how Central Banks, through open market operations, increase money supply by buying assets to financial intermediaries.

[9] Recall the money supply measures we have seen in chapter 2.

[10] Recall we defined moral hazard in section 2.5 as 'any situation in which one person makes the decision about how much risk to take, while someone else bears the cost if things go badly'. See Krugman (2009).

(CDS) that had been used as insurance. The American authorities believed that if AIG fell, a large stake of the global financial system would be affected by new losses they believed insured, provoking new bankruptcies such that the potential chain reaction would lead to the eventual total collapse of the financial system. On September 16th, 2008, the Federal Reserve rescued AIG through the issuance of an $85 billion credit facility.

The first truly financial panic—so far mostly limited to the U.S. market—broke during these hours. A 'flight to liquidity' of never-seen proportions and velocity took place: so much money fled from all types of investments (stock markets, bonds, deposits...) to U.S. Treasury Bills—allegedly the safest asset in the world—that its return felt to nearly 0% while interest rates on the interbank market raised sharply. This increased the U.S. Treasuries—Eurodollar spread—known as the TED spread, the best indicator of perceived counterparty risk in the interbank market—to near 500 basis points, when before 2007 the normal average level was about 20 to 50.

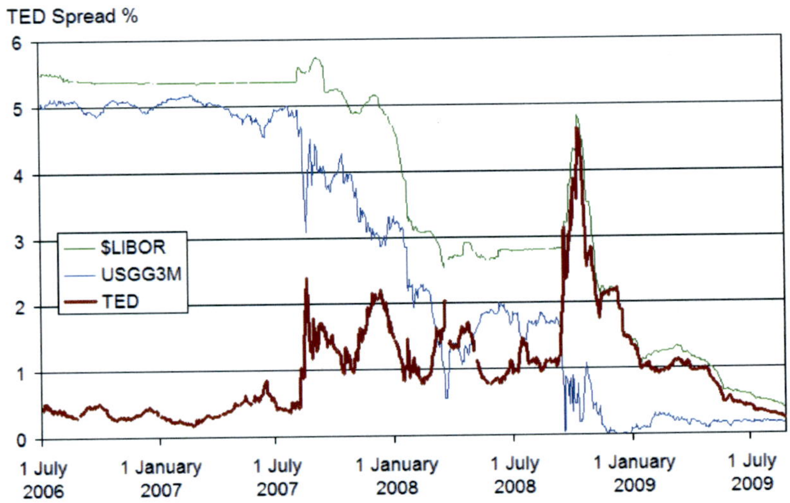

Figure 39. U.S. Treasuries - Eurodollar (TED) spread.

That data convinced the liberal American authorities that the only thing that could be done to save the situation was pure and simple interventionism: a $700 billion rescue plan for the financial system was approved. Since orthodox—even though to a large scale—measures of flooding markets with liquidity (money for 'healthy' fixed income securities) did not stop the bleeding, the rescue plan proposed the same idea, but buying the 'toxic assets' instead. A myth had fallen: likewise the 2001 terrorist attacks on the twin towers overthrew the idea of an U.S. untouchable in its territory, with this intervention the myth of an unwavering financial system, motor of decades of successfully capitalism, fell down.

For several days there were moments of relative calm. Nevertheless, soon data coming from Europe suggested that maybe subprime mortgages had been sold in California, but a large stake of them had been bought by European banks. The first victims begun to fall also in Europe, the contagion of the crisis spread all throughout the world at all levels, and worldwide panic probably reached its peak during the first half of October 2008, when stock markets around the world fell to their minimum levels in more than a decade.

Chapter 14

THE GREAT RECESSION (AFTER THE GREAT MODERATION)

Those weeks during September and October 2008 represented the peak of the financial crisis. We still have witnessed some episodes of panic later on, like during the Greek sovereign debt crisis and the fears it triggered on the sustainability of other E.U. countries' debt, and even on the Eurozone economic and monetary integration model itself. But two years after Lehman Brothers collapse we may say that though the consequences of the financial crisis maybe are not totally over, they seem to have eased up to some extent.

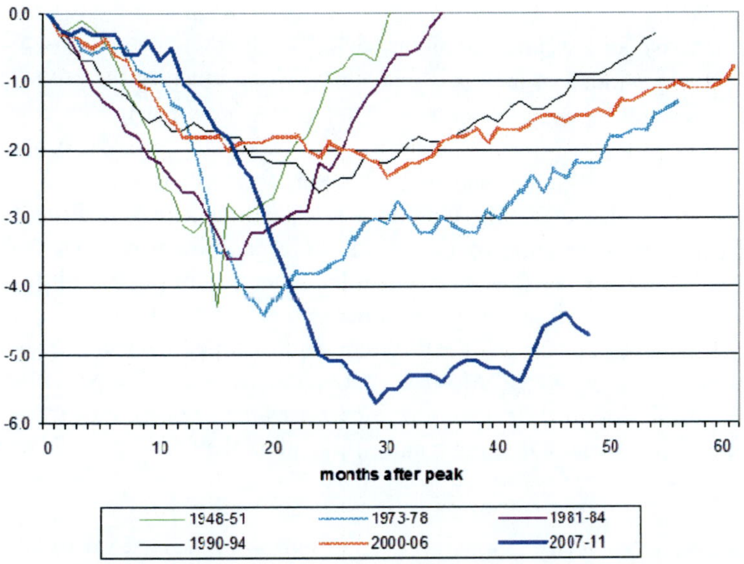

Source: Bureau of Labour Statistics.

Figure 40. U.S. unemployment rate: Recovery cycles[1].

[1] We also recommend our readers to have a look at the 'Employment recession comparison chart for the U.S. economy', a figure drawn by Amanda Cox and published at The New York Times by Catherine Rampell. In

On the contrary, those days also represented the start of the greatest global economic contraction during peacetime in almost a century. It seems anyway we have been lucky—we have also been smart—because at first the fear of the unknown, the scaring possibility that the whole banking system could have collapsed, and the expectative that the financial crisis might cause large negative effects made many analysts think that the global economy could enter into a long period of economic squeezing like the Great Depression in the 1930s. Now that threat seems gone due to huge unconventional fiscal and monetary countercyclical policies by economic authorities around the globe. However, both in terms of economic growth and employment contraction (see figure 40) this crisis is being so destructive that it exceeds any other economic downturn in the past seventy years. That is the reason it has been named by some authors as the 'Great Recession'.

We differentiate two broad fields where consequences of this crisis have become more evident: doubts over the effectiveness of the global financial system, and the impact over the world's economy. The emergency required to avoid an economic depression (and probably that voters are more concerned about their economy than aware of the global financial system shortcomings) made governments soon forget the necessity of addressing the necessary reforms on global capital markets, but the academic world is boiling these days with debates about the effectiveness of monetary policies, the role of central banks, enhancing regulation on the private banking sector and many other topics.

14.1. CONSEQUENCES OVER THE FINANCIAL SYSTEM

Financial markets are essential for any model of the market economy we might think of, and so it is crucial for much of the good functioning—and much of the problems too, if not properly managed—of capitalist economies. That is the reason why this crisis, caused by faults on financial system, surprised almost everyone, especially when the banking sector had a brilliant reputation at that time, and when economic growth was beating all marks. The shock was so intense that even the appropriateness of letting private firms to govern the financial system and the creation of money in our economies was brought into question, especially when taking into consideration that at the time most of the American and European banks needed financial support, to the point of become nationalized some of them.

What has indeed become clear is the different nature of the financial industry with respect to other sectors of the economy. Most Western authorities had to rescue every bank in jeopardy with no exception, while with other enterprises they worked on a case by case basis, considering the effects over GDP growth and employment their failure would cause. They did so because, as we said,

> in any transaction money appears—in all of its forms—by the same value of the goods or services being traded. Indeed, commerce led to the emergence of financial markets, closely related to the real economy as a mirror image of it[2].

---

terms of unemployment they compare this crisis with past economic crisis in the U.S. As of June 2011 this crisis was clearly the worst crisis in the last five decades. Their analysis is regularly updated at <http://economix.blogs>.

[2] See section 1.1 in chapter 1.

The financial sector has then an equivalent size than the real economy, since any transaction of goods or services encompasses a cash flow in the opposite direction. Furthermore, the development of financial markets—and namely, the derivatives markets—expanded the universe of financial transactions to others of an exclusive 'virtual' nature, with no effect on the real economy.

No matter how many sub-sectors we might identify on the industry (banks, saving banks, credit cooperatives, insurance companies, asset management, pension funds, investment banking, private banking...) it is a fact that the financial sector is concentrated in just a few hands[3]. Before the financial meltdown, the expression 'too big to fail' portrayed the belief within the industry that bigger banks would had lower risk because, due to globalization, they had achieved a volume such that they could never default. Probably this reasoning reduced risk aversion and provoked the practices behind the origin of the present crisis, as we have seen. But once the crisis started, not only we found out that 'too big to fail' companies might, indeed, fail, but also that if they did, they could have a devastating effect over the economy, requiring authorities to intervene[4].

So now quite reasonable worries have arisen about whether it is acceptable for economic authorities that, literally, our economies are dependent on the good behaviour of just a few companies. Prime rule of free markets says *who takes risks must bear the consequences*, but the banking system seems not to follow that rule. Under this model, agents benefited from risky decisions when they become a success do not assume losses—or either are unable to assume them—when they fail. This idea, 'moral hazard', is for many analysts the ultimate explanation for what happened in Wall Street.

To sum up, this crisis represents a warning call on the necessity to go back to the origins of the financial system: it should return to be an instrument serving the real economy, *closely related to the real economy as a mirror image of it*. Instead, these last decades we assisted to the development of the financial sector as a business itself, *making money out of money*. And not only banks are responsible for that, but the whole society, where people from large investors to households with no experience at all in financial markets required high returns on investments they did not understand, or not willing to assume the risks they were facing.

It would be a mistake to rely on mono-causal explanations for this crisis, so there is still more. We should pay attention on topics like the global imbalances caused by a system where capital is allowed to move freely in a world with different accountant regimes, tax policies and fiscal havens (which were told to be banned shortly, but after two years—surprise!—nothing has changed). We should also analyze retail banking credit policies[5] that boosted credit all around the world, compel OTC derivatives to be executed in regulated markets with the intervention of a clearinghouse (something it is already being promoted), enhance banking regulation, and others. In general, as Bean (2010) points out, it seems the economics profession has oversold the virtues of unfettered financial markets. We

[3] As an empirical evidence, in the Spanish economy only two banks (Santander and BBVA) had in 2007-2008 the same income as the sum of all the other banks' income altogether, and only twenty entities, between banks and savings banks, accounted for almost the entirely industry income. See <www.cartascomerciales.es/banco/comisiones/rankingdebancos. html>.

[4] Ben Bernanke, on his testimony before the Financial Crisis Inquiry Commission about the 'Causes of the Recent Financial and Economic Crisis', has effusively pinpointed having allowed 'too big to fail' banks to exist as one of the most important causes of the crisis. See Bernanke (2010).

[5] See Peón and Calvo (2010) for further analysis of behavioural economics on retail banking credit policies and regulation.

need to bring psychology and behavioural economics into the study of financial markets, and we should also learn from history, because the frequency of financial booms and busts suggests we should think of them as a central feature of capitalist economies, an idea that has renewed interest in Hyman Minky's theory of endogenous financial instability[6].

Even though authorities have been more concerned about fighting the consequences of the financial meltdown over the real economy, when everything is over they should work on introducing the necessary adjustments in order to avoid it could happen again. Otherwise they will be required to justify why, after what has happened, they allow the financial system to continue the same way as before: accumulating profits during upturns, but unable to assume losses in downturns; inducing practices like moral hazard or predatory lending during good times, whose consequences are bored by other agents in the economy; and during recessions, they worsen things by restricting credit, reducing money supply when it is needed the most.

14.2. Consequences over the Economy

Right after the crisis hit our lives, the first concerns were about its duration and intensity, to the point that some feared that we could fall into a second Great Depression. But as soon as fiscal and monetary policies could handle the situation, doubts turned to which kind of recovery our economies would experience: V-shaped recovery, L-shaped recovery, W-shaped recovery, U-shaped recovery, and so on. So far it appears the world economy is in fact witnessing all those schedules at the same time, depending on which region we are focusing. It also seems there could be a correlation between recovery rates and debt ratios during the previous years. This way, China, Brazil, or Germany, for example, could be performing a V recovery, whereas countries like Portugal, Italy, Ireland, Greece and Spain are facing a real menace of an economic stagnation.

We started part III setting the origins of the present crisis at the end of the ideological confrontation between capitalism and communism. Now, during the last months, a new debate has been raised between defenders of the role of the State as a savior of market economies during crisis, acting as a countercyclical agent, and those who argue that massive indebtedness by States could provoke an ultimate, more virulent, episode of this crisis. Could we think of this as the origin of a new era of ideological confrontation, a sort of revival between Keynesian and Neoliberal ideas?

The debate is right now at its climax, so from our point of view it would be more prudent to shed some light about the nature of this indebtedness and the effects it has over economic growth. Authors like Reinhart and Rogoff (2010), for example, provided a measure of historical debt level in the U.S.[7]. In figure 38 (see chapter 13) we have also depicted the U.S. total debt over GDP ratio, which clearly seems not sustainable over the long term. Since 2001—when a historical new record, already above the Great Depression level, was achieved—we entered into a second stage that boosted indebtedness to unseen marks around 400% of GDP. In other words, U.S. citizens—government, households and firms—had at that

[6] See Minsky (1982).

[7] In figure 41 we have drawn U.S. total debt over GDP starting from1959. Readers can find further data in Reinhart and Rogoff (2010), where data from early 20th century are provided.

time spent more than four years of future income. Today U.S. total debt accounts for about \$57 trillion, three and a half times the U.S. GDP!

On the other hand, it should be noted that the public sector is sometimes blamed from misbehaviours actually coming from households and private institutions, as it happens for example in Spain or Ireland, or generally speaking in the E.U.[8] There, government debt accounts for a decreasing ratio of debt to GDP during the last ten years (about a reasonable level of 60% in 2008), whereas corporations and households account for more than 300%. Banks' debt should not be added in order to avoid double accounting, but it is also worth mention their increasing debt exposure during the years previous to the meltdown (about 50% of GDP in just three years), which in our opinion enlightens the massive off-balance sheet practices and the necessity of higher capital requirements within the industry.

Finally, Reinhart and Rogoff (2010) have also studied the potential damages debt would have caused on GDP growth during the last century and across different countries. They found that[9]

> the relationship between government debt and real GDP growth is weak for debt/GD rations below 90% of GDP. Above the threshold of 90% median growth rates fall by 1%, and average growth falls considerably more. The threshold for public debt is similar in advanced and emerging economies.

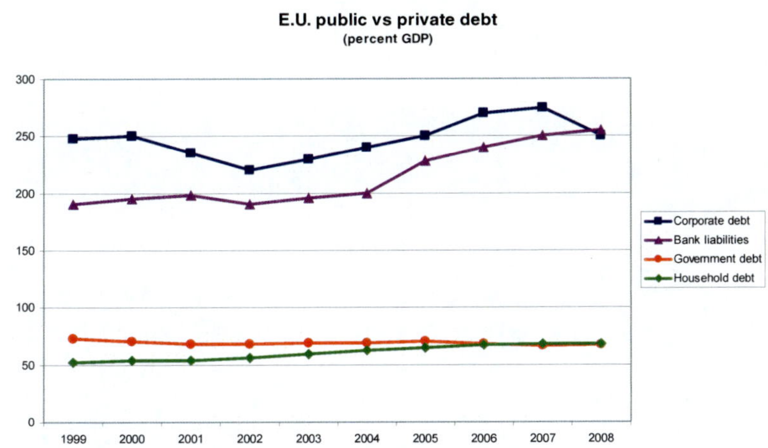

Source: Based on De Grauwe (2010).

Figure 41. E.U. government vs. private debt.

It seems that the level of 60% mentioned before for the E.U. as a whole would have no negative effects over the economy. The debate about the sustainability of government debt will remain, anyway, still open. For how much time? We have not the answer.

---

[8] See De Grauwe (2010).

[9] Reinhart and Rogoff (2010).

REFERENCES

Akerlof, G.A. (1970), The market for 'lemons': Quality uncertainty and the market mechanism, *Quarterly Journal of Economics* 84, 488-500.

Aliber, R.Z. (1973), The interest rate parity theorem: A reinterpretation, *Journal of Political Economy* 81, 1451-59.

Amat, O. (2000), *La Bolsa. Funcionamiento y técnicas para invertir*, Bilbao: Deusto.

Antelo, M. and D. Peón (2011), Productos financieros y perfil del inversor: de la práctica a la teoría, in *Ahorro Familiar en España*, Madrid: Papeles de la Fundación de Estudios Financieros 39.

Arrow, K.J., and G. Debreu (1951), Existence of an equilibrium for a competitive economy, *Econometrica* 22, 265-290.

Ball, R. (1994), The development, accomplishment and limitations of the theory of Stock Market Efficiency, *Management Finance* 20, 3-47.

Bean, Ch. (2010), The great moderation, the great panic and the great contraction, *Journal of the European Economic Association* 8, 289-325.

Bernanke, B. (2010), Causes of the recent financial and economic crisis, testimony before the Financial Crisis Inquiry Commission, Washington D.C. Available at <http://www.federalreserve.gov/newsevents/testimony/bernanke20100902a.htm>.

Black, F. and M. Scholes (1973), The Pricing of Options and Corporate Liabilities, *Journal of Political Economy* 81, 637-654.

Blake, D. (2000), *Financial Market Analysis*. Chichester: John Wiley & Sons(2nd edition).

Brealey, R.A. and Myers, S.C. (2003), *Principles of Corporate Finance*, London: McGraw Hill (7th edition).

Buiter, W. (2009), The wonderful world of negative nominal interest rates, again. Working Paper at VoxEU.org. Available at <www.voxeu.org/index.php?q=node/3626>.

De Grauwe, P. (2010), Fighting the wrong enemy, Working Paper at VoxEU.org. Available at <www.voxeu.org/index.php?q=node/5062>.

Domowitz, I. (1993), A taxonomy of automated trade execution systems, *Journal of International Money and Finance* 12, 607-631.

Elliot, R.N. (1938), The Wave Principle, in R.R. Prechter, Jr. (ed.), *R.N. Elliott's Masterworks. The Definitive Collection*, New York: New Classics Library (1st edition.1994).

Elton, E.J. and M.J. Gruber (1977), Risk reduction and portfolio size: An analytical solution, *Journal of Business* 50, 415-437.

Fama, E.F. (1965), Random walks in stock market prices, *Financial Analysis Journal* 21, 55-59.

Fama, E.F. (1970), Efficient capital markets: A review of theory and empirical work, *Journal of Finance* 25, 383-417.

Fisher, I. (1911), *The Purchasing Power of Money: Its Determination and Relation to Credit, Interest and Crises*, New York: Macmillan (1st Edition, 1922).

Freixas, X. and J.C. Rochet (1997), *Microeconomics of Banking*, Cambridge, Mass.: The MIT Press.

Goodhart, C. and D. Tsomocos (2010), Liquidity, default and market regulation, Working Paper at VoxEU.org. Available at <www.voxeu.org/index.php?q=node/4189>.

Hens, T. and K. Bachmann (2008), *Behavioral Finance for Private Banking*, New York: John Wiley & Sons.

Hull, J.C. (2000), *Options, futures and other derivatives*, London: Prentice Hall (fourth edition).

Jabbour, G.M. and P.H. Budwick (2010), *The Option Trader Handbook: Strategies and Trade Adjustments*, New York: John Wiley & Sons.

Jensen, M. (1978), Some anomalous evidence regarding market efficiency, *Journal of Financial Economics* 6, 95-101.

Kahneman, D. and A. Tversky (1979), Prospect theory: An analysis of decision under risk, *Econometrica* 47, 263-291.

Kindleberger, Ch. and R. Aliber (2005), *Manias, Panics and Crashes. A History of Financial Crisis*, New York: John Wiley & Sons.

Krugman, P. (2000), Thinking about the liquidity trap, *Journal of the Japanese and International Economies* 14, 221-237.

Krugman, P. (2009), *The Return of Depression Economics and the Crisis of 2008*, New York: W.W. Norton.

Lintner, J.V. (1965), The valuation of risk assets and the selection of risky investments in stock portfolios and capital budgets, *Review of Economics and Statistics* 47, 13-37.

López de Prado, M.M. and C. Rodrigo-Illera (2005), *Invertir en Hedge Funds*, Madrid: Díaz de Santos.

Malkiel, B.G. (2003), *A Random Walk down Wall Street: The Time-tested Strategy for Succesful Investing,* New York: W.W. Norton (completely revised and updated edition).

Mankiw, G. (2009), Reloading the weapons of monetary policy, Working Paper at Greg Mankiw's blog. Available at <gregmankiw.blogspot.com/2009/03/reloading-weapons-of-monetary-policy.html>

Markowitz, H.M. (1952), Portfolio selection, *Journal of Finance* 7, 77-91.

Martín-Marín, J.L. and R.J. Ruíz-Martínez (1991), *El Inversor y los mercados financieros*, Barcelona: Ariel.

Merton, R.C. (1973), Theory of rational option pricing, *Bell Journal of Economics and Management Science* 4 (1), 141–183

Minsky, H. (1982), The financial-instability hypothesis: Capitalist processes and the behavior of the economy. In Ch. Kindleberger and J.P. Laffargue (eds.), *Financial Crises*, Cambridge: Cambridge University Press.

Mossin, J. (1966), Equilibrium in a capital asset market, *Econometrica* 34, 768-783.

Peón, D. and A. Calvo (2010), Using behavioral economics to analyze credit policies on the banking industry, mimeo, Universidade da Coruña.

Pisón, I. (2001), *Dirección y gestión financiera de la empresa*, Madrid: Pirámide.

Reinhart, C. and K. Rogoff (2009), *This Time is Different. Eight Centuries of Financial Folly*, Princeton: Princeton University Press.

Reinhart, C. and K. Rogoff (2010), Debt and growth revisited, Working paper at VoxEU.org. Available at <www.voxeu.org/index.php?q=node/5395>.

Roll, R. (1977), A critique of the asset pricing theory's tests, *Journal of Financial Economics* 4, 129-176.

Ross, S. (1976), The arbitrage theory of capital asset pricing, *Journal of Economic Theory* 13, 341-360.

Sharpe, W.F. (1963), A simplified model for portfolio analysis, *Management Science* 9, 277-293.

Sharpe, W.F. (1964), Capital asset prices – A theory of market equilibrium under conditions of risk, *Journal of Finance* 19, 425-442.

Shastri, R. (2010), Beyond the zero lower bound on interest rates, Working Paper at VoxEU.org. Available at <www.voxeu.org/index.php?q=node/5407>.

Shefrin, H. (2002), *Beyond Greed and Fear. Understanding Behavioral Finance and the Psychology of Investing*, Oxford: Oxford University Press.

Shiller, R.J. (2000), *Irrational exhuberance*, Princeton: Princeton University Press.

Shleifer, A. (2000), *Inefficient Markets. An Introduction to Behavioural Finance*, Oxford: Oxford University Press.

Statman, M. (1987), How many stocks make a diversified portfolio?, *Journal of Financial and Quantitative Analysis* 22, 353-363.

Statman, M. (1999), Behavioral Finance: Past Battles, Future Engagements, *Financial Analysts Journal*, 55 (6), 18-27.

Stein, J. (1962), The nature and efficiency of the foreign exchange market, *Essays in International Finance*, No. 40, Princeton University.

Taylor, J.B. (1993), Discretion versus policy rules in practice, *Carnegie-Rochester Conference Series on Public Policy* 39, 195-214.

Tobin, J. (1958), Liquidity preference as behavior towards risk, *Review of Economics Studies* 26, 65-86.

Treynor, J.L. (1961), Market value, time and risk, Unpublished manuscript dated 8/8/61. Renamed as Treynor, J.L. (1962), Toward a theory of market value of risky assets, mimeo, subsequently published in Korajczyk, R.A. (1999), *Asset Pricing and Portfolios Performance: Models Strategy and Performance Metrics*, London: Risk Books

Treynor, J.L. (1965), How to rate management of investment funds, *Harvard Business Review* 43, 63-75.

About the Authors

Manel Antelo is Associate Professor of Economics at the University of Santiago de Compostela (Spain). He has taken part in eight competitive research projects, and is the author of five books and numerous articles in leading economic journals. Recently, he has written *Portions of Economics*. Besides, he is also part of the team of experts of the Spanish National Agency of Evaluation and Prospective.

David Peón is Assistant Professor of Finance at the University of A Coruña (Spain) and employee of BBVA Group. MSc in Finance by Birkbeck College (University of London) and CFA charterholder, his professional experience includes working as a portfolio manager at BBVA Private Banking in A Coruña, and as a market analyst at BBVA Asset Management in Madrid. Author of several research projects and articles in leading journals, his research interests include portfolio management, banking and behavioral finance.

INDEX

V

Y